S0-BCR-678

To Patrick,

Wishing you many...

Moments of Magic

Shep M... 2017

MOMENTS
of
MAGIC

Praise for *Moments of Magic*

"*Moments of Magic* is a clearly written, specific guide to making the best of customer contact situations. At a time when customers are more demanding than ever, this is excellent, hands-on advice for those serving on the front line."

—Michael LeBoeuf, Author of *How to Win Customers and Keep Them for Life*

"*Moments of Magic* should be on every manager's bookshelf. It addresses the biggest challenge facing business today, making customers a number one priority. Anyone involved in business would benefit from its powerful message."

—Thomas A. Pall, Vice President Sales, Southwestern Bell Yellow Pages

"We all have those *Moments of Magic*, when everything is just right. This book provides an empowering philosophy that will help you prepare for those moments."

—Robert Young, Vice President Trade Development, Energizer Battery Company

"No sleight-of-hand, no hocus pocus, no smoke-and-mirrors! *Moments of Magic* offers straightforward advice about how to delight, not just satisfy, your customers. And Shep Hyken's insightful, entertaining stories delight, not just satisfy, his readers."

—Mark Tucker, Vice President Performance Improvement Training, Maritz, Inc.

"You have provided easy-to-read, easy-to-understand instructions to create our own *Moments of Magic*. This book is a must read on my recommended list!"

—Ty Boyd, Author of *Visions*

"This is the book you have been waiting for! Short, simple, superb. Solid information for every business and useful instruction for every individual. Shep Hyken has definitely put together a winner, and I highly recommend it."

—Nido Qubein, President, High Point University

"Every one of our convenience store managers and employees must create *Moments of Magic*. We have to build relationships with our customers if we want them to come back again and again. The ideas in this book are right on target for everyone from upper management to the store employees."

—Scott Gabriele, Vice President Corporate Marketing, Circle K Corporation

Praise for *The Loyal Customer*

"The typical business loses half of their customers every 48 months. The companies that create the most value keep the business. Read this lesson and rediscover the word SERVICE and what it really means."

—Tom Pall, Vice President Sales, SBC Directory Operations

"Shep not only spins an entertaining tale of a cab driver who takes customer service to new levels, but he helps the reader develop a clear blueprint on how to improve service in their own business."

—Rick Snyder, Senior Vice President, Enterprise Rent-a-Car

Praise for *The Cult of the Customer*

"At Zappos.com, we recognize that customers need to be more than satisfied—they need to be WOWed! Shep recognizes this as well in his book, and gives examples of how different companies go about creating WOW experiences."

—Tony Hsieh, CEO, Zappos.com

"Ultimately, we want loyal customers—not just loyal to our brand, but also to our dealerships. This book teaches how to get customers, in any business, to come back again and again."

—Mike Rencis, Customer Service Operations, Toyota Motor Sales, USA

Praise for *The Amazement Revolution*

"Practical, tactical, and hands-on, this book will push you to initiate the customer interactions you should have been doing all along."

—Seth Godin, Author, *Poke the Box*

"In reading Shep Hyken's *The Amazement Revolution*, I applaud his approach. At American Express, we view service not as a cost, but as an investment in building customer relationships. Through Relationship Care—our overarching service ethos—we strive to emotionally connect with our customers and add value to every interaction. The seven strategies outlined in this book are exactly how we operate."

—James P. Bush, Executive Vice President, World Service, American Express

Books by Shep Hyken

The Loyal Customer: A Lesson from a Cab Driver

Only the Best on Success (co-author)

Only the Best on Customer Service (co-author)

Only the Best on Leadership (co-author)

The Winning Spirit (co-author)

Inspiring Others to Win (co-author)

*The Cult of the Customer: Create an Amazing Experience that
Turns Satisfied Customers into Customer Evangelists*

*The Amazement Revolution: Seven Customer Service Strategies
to Create an Amazing Customer (and Employee) Experience*

For more information about the above books contact:

Shepard Presentations, LLC
(314) 692-2200
info@hyken.com
www.hyken.com

MOMENTS
of
MAGIC

SHEP HYKEN

The Alan Press

Moments of Magic®

A Shepard Presentation

All rights reserved.

Copyright © 1993, 2002, 2012 by Shep Hyken.

Moments of Magic®, Moments of Misery™ are trademarks of Shep Hyken, Shepard Presentations, LLC. All rights reserved.

For ordering information or special discounts for bulk purchases, please contact Shepard Presentations, LLC at (314) 692-2200 or http://www.Hyken.com.

This book may not be reproduced in whole or in part, by any other means or using any technology, without permission. For information contact:

(314) 692-2200

Email: shep@hyken.com

Published by The Alan Press

http://www.hyken.com

Library of Congress Catalog Number: 2012909883

ISBN: 978-0-9637820-2-1

Printed in the United States of America

10 9 8 7 6 5 4

Table of Contents

About the Book xi

Introduction xiii

1. *The Moment of Magic* 1

PART I: *What It Takes To Make Magic*

2. *Make a Positive Impression* 21
3. *Know Your Business* 27
4. *Be Informed: Know a Little About a Lot* 35
5. *Be Enthusiastic* 39
6. *Understand Your Customer* 47

PART II: *Ways to Create Moments of Magic*

7. *Provide Quality at Every Turn* 59
8. *Respond Quickly* 67
9. *Solve Their Problems* 73
10. *Be Reliable* 81
11. *Appreciate Your Customer* 89

PART III: *Putting Moments of Magic to Work*

12. *Handling the Complaining Customer* 99
13. *Building a Team Spirit of Service* 117
14. *Conclusion* 131

Recommended Reading 139

About This Book
(Preface to the Second Edition)

You are reading the revised and updated edition of *Moments of Magic*. The first edition of the book was published way back in 1993 and was conceived long before then. That means this updated version now spans more than two decades of customer focused experience in helping companies deliver world-class customer service.

When this book was first written, the newfangled concepts of the "World Wide Web" and the Internet had only recently been introduced. If you had ever heard of something called a "web page," it was because you were an engineer or programmer of some kind. A lot has changed since then!

In bringing this book into the 21st century, I've been struck by how quickly and radically our communication technologies can change. For instance, as of this writing (2012), one of the dominant communication platforms, and one that I love using, is Twitter. As I write these words, though, I realize that no one can say for sure how long Twitter will hold on to its current position of dominance.

Even so, I have revised this book on the assumption that Twitter will be around for a while ... at least until I get around to a third edition of this book. You will see as you make your way through the book that I have included Tweetable, 140-characters-or-less summaries of key points at the end of each main section. These summaries appear under the heading "*Magic Hints!*" Please share these concise insights online via Twitter, Facebook, LinkedIn, Google+, or any other portal you frequent—and please also be sure to include my website, www.Hyken.com, at the end of the message. Speaking of the website, at the end of each chapter, I have also included web links to relevant articles, videos, and more.

You can explore the topics covered in greater depth at: www.MomentsOfMagicBook.com.

For example, check out your first Magic Hint!

Visit www.MomentsOfMagicBook.com/magic-hints

Or Scan:

Enjoy!

P.S. Please let me know what you think of this book. There are lots of ways for us to stay connected...

- Follow me on Twitter: @Hyken
- Like me on Facebook: www.facebook.com/ShepHykenSpeaker
- Connect on LinkedIn: www.linkedin.com/in/shephyken
- Join me on Google+: Just search for "Shep Hyken"
- Watch me on YouTube: www.YouTube.com/shephyken
- Read my blog: www.CustomerServiceBlog.com
- Visit my website: www.Hyken.com

Introduction

People ask me all the time, "How did *Moments of Magic* come to be?"

I'll tell you. The first speech I ever developed was a motivational speech titled "You Are The Magic!" It mixed important messages with humor and magic. I started using the phrase "Moments of Magic" to define everything that was good. In 1987, I read one of the greatest books on service ever written, Jan Carlzon's *Moments of Truth*. That book inspired me to turn my general motivational speech into a much more powerful business presentation, one focused on the elements of truly outstanding service. This was during an era when a lot of businesses were just talking about customer service, and very few were actually making superior customer service a strategic priority. And Carlzon's *Moments of Truth* and my Moments of Magic was a perfect combination.

So the research began. I bought every book the bookstores had to offer in the areas of quality and service. At the time, I was working for many clients and had numerous opportunities to interview executives and experience for myself how different companies viewed quality and service issues.

Then, one fateful day I found myself working with professional speaker and author Phil Wexler, who specializes in service and sales. Phil and I share very similar business philosophies, especially in the area of service. He told me of his own concept of creating "Moments of Magic" – a presentation originating from, you guessed it, Jan Carlzon's work. I told him how I also talked about Carlzon's theories and how I used magic tricks to help back up the important points (the same way other speakers might tell stories or jokes). We knew right away that we were speaking the same language.

It hit us both at the same time. I used magic in my speeches and talked about creating Moments of Magic. And the tie-in with

Carlzon's *Moments of Truth* was a perfect combination. Thanks to Phil, I had a new twist in my speech. As always, I would weave in the information, stories, and even magic tricks, but I would add this one important phrase...

"Moments of Magic!"

This book, which is built around that concept, is meant for everyone, in every occupation, in every business. Its concepts are timeless and will work whether you are the president, the secretary or the mail clerk. One of the important truths that businesses are finally becoming aware of is that *everyone is involved in service.* You might be a CEO or a bus driver or an assembly line worker. It doesn't matter. You serve someone. And since you serve someone, this book is meant for you, no matter what your job title is.

The emphasis here is on relationship building and meeting the expectations of the people you work with and sell to. And, as an added bonus, much of this information will work in your personal life as well.

The goal of this book is to get you to think about quality service at all times. Quality service is not a department or job description. It is an attitude. It is the way we have to do business.

CHAPTER 1

The Moment of Magic

"Houdini said: 'There is no trick getting the rabbit out of the hat; the real trick is getting him in there in the first place.' There is a similar law of life, that there is no trick getting success out of any of us; the real trick is getting within us the dedication, desire and perseverance that lead to success."

—Cavett Robert

- How many times have you walked into a restaurant for a meal and found the service and food so outstanding that you left an extra large tip and pledged to return again soon?
- Have you ever had the experience of working with repair people who fix your car or your house right the first time, charge a fair price and explain what they are doing…so that you want to speak highly of them and recommend them to others?
- Have you ever been in the hospital and had nurses who seemed cheerful and caring, who did special things to lift your spirits toward a faster recovery?
- Have you stayed in hotels where all the staff seemed courteous and helpful and truly made you feel like a VIP?

- Are there departments or people in your business on whom you can always depend for help, who promptly give you what you need and do so with a smile?
- When you talk to your boss, does he or she give you full attention, respect and encouragement?

All of these are examples of what I call *Moments of Magic.*

When you have been treated to a Moment of Magic, you feel extra satisfaction, knowing that someone has gone the extra mile to serve you. A Moment of Magic is what happens when you receive above average service, especially when you are accustomed to average service. A Moment of Magic is getting something extra without paying for more. A Moment of Magic is a personal touch, knowing that someone cared enough to see that your work was done well.

No matter what business or occupation you are in, you can use the Moments of Magic concept to achieve greater success in your line of work.

When you create Moments of Magic, your customers will want to do business with you again and again. And they will tell all their friends to do business with you.

We're in Business to Serve Our Customers

Let me ask you a question: What is the function of your business?

Most people when asked this question answer, "To make money."

But then I ask them to distinguish between the function and the goal of a business. Yes, the goal of a business is to make money, or in the case of a non-profit organization, to fulfill its mission.

The function of a business is what its people do in their jobs, day in and day out. Make money? Yes, ultimately.

But consider these wise words from Dr. Theodore Levitt, senior professor at Harvard Business School:

**"The function of every business and organization
is to get and keep customers."**

No matter who you are or what you do, you have customers. You may call them patrons, buyers, clients, patients, tenants, volunteers, members, students, donors, faculty, staff, associates, partners, employees or any number of other names.

Whatever you call your customer, you have people whom you serve; people who buy your product or service...most often, with money. Some customers, though, buy the product by giving their time. These include members of churches, service clubs and other volunteer organizations.

Employees, who are the internal customers, buy the product by giving their allegiance and hard work to the employer.

You depend on the customer for your living. You must understand your customer and what he or she wants.

Without customers, your business is dead. If you fail to satisfy your customers, they will walk away to the competition, or just not buy at all. The single most important task your business faces each day is getting and keeping customers.

IMPORTANCE OF SERVICE

Good customer service is critical to business success. Ron Zemke, co-author of the classic *Service America*, reminded us that 72 percent of our jobs and 68 percent of the Gross National Product lie in the service sector.

In a Gallup Poll survey of 600 executives of Fortune 500 companies, the majority said that service will be the most important element to help them stay ahead of the competition. Most of the others felt that dealing with change would be the most important element. Perhaps they meant change in the way they deal with customers and how they can meet customers' changing expectations.

INTERNAL CUSTOMERS AND EXTERNAL CUSTOMERS

"I don't deal directly with the public, so my job doesn't involve customer service."

Wrong!

Every job in a company has an impact, directly or indirectly, on customer service. To understand why this is so, you must understand that there are two types of customers: internal customers and external customers. The external customer is the buyer of your company's product or service. But it's just as important to remember that within any company or organization, you also have many internal customers. Internal customers are the people in the next department with whom you work. An internal customer is the vice president for whom you do a special project, the employees in your department who you want to build into a happy, productive team, the board of directors and, of course, perhaps the most important internal customer of all...your boss.

In a business, many people depend on each other to get their jobs done. Accounting, sales and production all need each other. The secretary serves the boss by completing assigned responsibilities. The boss serves the secretary by providing a favorable working environment, constructive feedback and a commitment to helping him or her do the best job he or she can.

If you don't think you have customers, consider this question: If you stopped doing your job for a week, who would notice?

Anyone who would notice is your customer. If no one notices, then your job is not having an impact on the company...and the job may be (and probably should be!) eliminated.

In *Service America*, Ron Zemke and Karl Albrecht write:

> **"If you're not serving the customer, you'd better be**
> **serving someone who is."**

In today's world, your enterprise is flirting with disaster if you think that the customer service department is the only area involved in customer service. Everyone should be their own customer service department! Whether you are a clerk in the accounting department or a sales rep on the floor, you have customers, and you are involved in customer service.

MEETING THE CUSTOMER: THE MOMENT OF TRUTH

If the function of a business is to get and keep customers, how do we go about doing this? This is the big question. **Each time we interact with a customer (internal or external, virtually or person-to-person) we have the opportunity to make or break our business.**

Jan Carlzon, whom I've already mentioned as the author of *Moments of Truth,* was the president of Scandinavian Airlines, better known as SAS. The title of his book comes from his name for this interaction: the moment of truth between customer and business. Discussing this concept, Carlzon writes:

> **"Any time a customer comes into contact with any aspect of your business, however remote, they have an opportunity to form an impression."**

Carlzon says there are a few main moments of truth for an air traveler. Those moments include…

- at the curb when passengers pull up to check their bags;
- at the ticket counter when they purchase or confirm their tickets;
- when they board the plane;
- when they get off the plane; and
- at the baggage claim area when they pick up their bags.

Then there are many other moments of truth that happen in between. You could be walking down the concourse toward the gate and pass an employee of the airline with which you're traveling. If he or she smiles at you, that could be a positive moment of truth. If you get a frown instead, that could be a negative moment. These are very subtle moments of truth than can and do make a difference.

Carlzon wrote that in a year, each of the company's 10 million customers come into contact with approximately five Scandinavian Airlines employees. Thus, the company has 50 million moments of truth with its customers each year. Each of these contacts lasts an average of just fifteen seconds!

Any moment of truth can go well or it can go poorly. When a moment of truth is great, I call it a Moment of Magic. A negative moment of truth is a Moment of Misery. Our job is to take all those moments of truth, and turn them into Moments of Magic.

Moments of truth can be big. But they are also the little things we do all day. For example, the way we answer the phone creates an impression. I might answer simply and abruptly, "This is Shep." Or, I could be more enthusiastic and say, "Good morning. This is Shep. How may I help you?" Which way sounds better? Everything we do contributes to making Moments of Magic.

MOMENTS OF MISERY

Sometimes all does not go well. Here are some examples of Moments of Misery.

You are driving to the grocery store. You notice a delivery truck pull behind the store, and men start to unload lettuce from it. You look at this delivery truck. It is the dirtiest, grimiest truck you have ever seen. If the outside of the truck is dirty, you must wonder what the inside looks like. You begin to have doubts about whether to buy lettuce or anything else from that store.

Or, you sit down in a restaurant. At your table, you notice dirt and pieces of food on the tablecloth and dirt on the glassware. When the meal comes, you notice something on the plate that looks like it does not belong there. Would you want to finish that meal, or return to that restaurant?

For me, a Moment of Misery came when I visited a hospital

lab for a blood test. Getting a blood test is not my favorite thing to do, and I especially do not like it when they prick my finger with a needle. My encounter with this hospital started in the admitting department. The lady in admitting asked me in a cold, terse voice for my name, address, telephone number and all sorts of other information. I tried but could not get this lady to crack a smile. She was downright scary. It's too bad because she is on the front line for the hospital. Even though her title might have just been receptionist, she is a public relations specialist for the hospital. Unfortunately, she was unaware of this fact.

After finishing with the lady in admitting, I was almost ready to just walk away. It was such a negative experience – it actually scared me for the trip to the lab. Going to a hospital is usually not an enjoyable experience for most people. I am glad I was not really sick or in an emergency. I would hate to have to deal with people like her during a time of pain.

Those are all examples of Moments of Misery. I'll bet you can think of a few of your own.

MOMENT OF MISERY BECOMES A MOMENT OF MAGIC

One of my favorite service examples has to do with a cab driver I encountered while on a trip to Dallas.

It was the middle of the summer, the temperature was about 99 degrees and the humidity was almost as high. It was hot. I walked out of the Dallas Convention Center looking for a cab. I carried two heavy bags on my way to the airport to catch a flight.

Up pulled a cab. The driver jumped out, and I saw he was wearing cutoff jeans filled with holes. He had on a sleeveless shirt, with tattoos on his arms. He had not shaven for a week. His hair was a mess and his T-shirt had a radical joke written across the front.

Looking at this guy, I was thinking that this was definitely going to be a Moment of Misery. It was going to take me at least 25 minutes to get to the airport, which meant I was going to have to ride with this guy for 25 minutes! Looking at him, I imagined how hot, smelly and dirty his cab was going to be.

Here was where the surprise began. In a mild mannered voice he said, "Sit down in the cab, sir; it's nice and cool. I'll take care of your bags."

I did what he said and started to get inside the cab. When I opened the door, cool air hit me. The cab was spotless. In the middle of the cab there was a bucket with ice and two soft drinks. I looked down at the seat and there was a copy of *USA Today* and a local Dallas newspaper. Then I noticed he had left a cell phone within easy reach.

When he got in the cab, he said, "Have a soft drink. Use the phone if you need to make a call."

I asked him if this was his cab, or if he was borrowing it for the day. He assured me it was his cab. Then he offered me a piece of candy.

He asked where I was going, and I told him: to the airport.

He flipped down the flag on the meter. At that time in Dallas, the cabs had a flat rate from downtown to the airport. When he flipped down the meter, I thought he was trying to rip me off. I knew from experience that the meter is always higher than the flat rate. Then, before I had the chance to say a thing, he said, "Sir, I'm flipping down the meter just to show you how much money you save with this flat rate."

My eyes lit up. I thought, this guy is much sharper than he looks. He's a salesman!

When we got on the highway, he asked another question: "Are you in a hurry or is it okay if I do the speed limit?"

"Just take your time," I said. As I drank the soda and read the newspaper, I wondered to myself just what kind of cab driver this was. I had never experienced a cab ride like this before.

We reached a certain point on the highway where there was a fork in the road. Either direction would take us to the airport in about equal time. He said if we went to the right, it would take us through Las Colinas, where there was the most beautiful fountain. He asked whether I had a few minutes to spare, because if I did, he wanted to take me to see it, and he would not charge anything extra since it was a flat rate. I humored him and agreed to go.

Soon we reached the fountain in Las Colinas. And it was indeed beautiful. It had huge, larger-than-life-size statues of mustangs galloping across the water. Where their hoofs hit the water, fountains sprayed up, as if the hoofs were splashing in the water. It really was the most beautiful fountain I had ever seen. You could see how proud he was of it.

We got back into the cab and headed back on our way to the airport. He asked for my business card. He said he collected the business cards of the people he drives. I gave him my card and he gave me his. He said to call him the next time I was in Dallas. He would pick me up at the airport, even meet me at the gate, and give me "limousine service at taxicab rates."

The fare was $22, but I paid $30 to give him a nice tip. It was a great ride. A Moment of Magic.

But that's not all! As the late, great broadcaster Paul Harvey used to say, "And now…the rest of the story."

Four days later, I was back in my office in St. Louis. I opened my mail and found a thank-you note from my cab driver, Frank Nelson. I was overwhelmed and, honestly, a little shocked. Who gets a thank-you note from a cab driver?

The note read, "I thank you for the opportunity to take you from the convention center to the airport. I hope you enjoyed the fountain."

Wow!

That thank-you note not only made my day…it made my week! I couldn't stop telling people about it.

Whenever I went to Dallas, I would call Frank. He would pick me up at the airport and take me anywhere I wanted to go. I told dozens, hundreds, probably thousands of people about him over the years. I remember clearly that, while working a convention in Dallas, I gave his name to three of my best clients. They used him…

and he took every one of them to see that fountain in Las Colinas. Here's the footnote. Months passed after my initial ride in Frank's car, and Christmas time came around. What did I get in the mail from Frank Nelson? You guessed it: a Christmas card! Frank Nelson told me that he treats his customers just the way he would want to be treated. His theory was that by doing this, he would make more money than any other cab driver in Dallas. And you know what? He was absolutely right!

MAGIC...A MOMENT THAT SPARKLES

There is a special reason I have chosen the term *Moments of Magic*.

Magic tricks are a classic way to dazzle an audience. Everyone enjoys a good magic trick. And magic has been an important part of my life since I was a boy.

I have been doing magic tricks since I was 10 years old. I found a book on card tricks and started practicing. By the time I was 12, I had learned many more tricks and started working birthday parties. At 14, I was doing magic tricks at nightclubs in Aspen, Colorado.

While in college, I decided on a serious career in the oil business. That lasted until the company was sold, two and a half years later.

Since 1983, I have been speaking professionally and using magic tricks as a part of my speech. Audiences love it because the tricks are an enjoyable way to help make an important point stand out in a memorable way.

There are many parallels between doing a magic act and providing good customer service. When you stand up in front of an audience, you want to put a smile on people's faces. You want to do something they enjoy. You do the same thing when you reach the customer. You give them a good experience, a positive experience, a great experience. You want to make sure the audience wants more. In the same way, you want to make sure the customer learns to expect the best.

Back when I was working nightclubs and banquets, I put a great deal of passion and enthusiasm into my magic show. That distinguished me from other magicians who had more raw ability and technical skill than I did. I was committed to doing a great job and giving the audience a good time. That passion showed through. While my ability was good, the passion and enthusiasm set me apart from the rest of the field. I knew my job was to entertain, not just do magic tricks.

In business, it is exactly the same. Everyone wants to take care of their customers, but some people care more and work harder at it than others. Good service can set a company ahead of competitors who have better products and less service. Showing that you care is of the utmost importance.

Going the extra mile in service creates magic for our customers and makes them want to come back again and again. In entertainment, a Moment of Magic is when you leave the audience wanting more. In business…

> **A Moment of Magic is a Moment of Truth – an interaction with an internal or external customer – that is simply, at a minimum, above average.**

THIRD TRY IS A MOMENT OF MAGIC

Years ago, my wife and I had the good fortune to buy a new home. That meant we had to sell our old home.

It took us a year and a half to sell the old one. We listed our home with two different agents, each of whom produced very little in the way of results. Over a year later, we had little activity and no offers. It was a nice house in a good location; nothing was wrong with it. It was just that the market was slow.

Things changed when we started working with Marilyn Singleton of Coldwell Banker. She was the fifth agent I interviewed. When we met, she gave me a binder with all sorts of information. There was a letter from the president of Coldwell Banker, saying how great Marilyn was and how she was one of their top agents.

The next page covered the listing agreement. Even though I had signed listing agreements twice previously (and watched as each expired without my house getting sold), Marilyn explained the agreement to me – and she did it in greater detail than the other two agents had. I learned plenty of things I didn't know before.

There was a special clause she added to the listing agreement. It impressed me, because it showed me just how much she believed in herself. Most listing agreements are for either three or six months. Marilyn inserted a clause that promised me that, if at any time I was not satisfied with her for any reason, I could cancel the listing, no questions asked.

Then there was the issue of price. Every single agent I had talked to had told me I had to lower my price. The market was down, and sellers were taking less.

Marilyn said the same thing…but what set Marilyn apart from the others was that she gave me information to back up her recommendation. The others simply shared the opinion that lowering the price would make the home sell. That was it. Marilyn gave me a computer analysis of all the comparable homes in my area that had been sold in the last year. She presented copies of information sheets on those homes, so we could compare them to mine, feature by feature. How many bedrooms? Finished basement? Fireplace? Updated kitchen and bathrooms? After all that, I had no problem lowering the price. Why? Because she gave me so many good reasons to set the price where we did, and she backed her recommendation up with solid information, not just an opinion.

Once I signed on with her, she continued to work hard. She made suggestions about sprucing up the house to make it more attractive. She offered to arrange for a lawn service and maids. She went to the house and supervised their work. Her lawn service was less expensive than the one I had been using! She or her assistant went to the house every other day, picking up newspapers, checking the mailbox, sprucing up and making sure the house was in tip-top shape.

Every week, she gave me a written report on all the shoppers who visited the house and what they liked and disliked about it.

Less than six weeks later, the house was sold. Marilyn Singleton had accomplished in six weeks what all the other agents could not achieve in over a year. She not only brought me one offer, she brought me two offers at the same time. She started a bidding war for the house!

When it came time to close, I had already planned to be on vacation. She knew I was going to be out of town, and arranged to have all the papers drawn up so I could pre-sign them before I left. She asked me for a deposit slip to my bank account, so the sale proceeds could be deposited directly into my account on the day of closing…while I was lying on a beach 2,000 miles away.

I have never experienced a level of professionalism and service comparable to what Marilyn Singleton delivered to us. Her attitude was, "I will take care of it; it's my job, I love what I do, and I want you to be happy."

Isn't it great when somebody takes that much pride in his or her job?

GOING THE EXTRA MILE

A few years back, I was giving a speech to staff members of Skywest Airlines, a commuter airline based in St. George, Utah. After my speech, the chairman of the board read the audience a letter he had received from a satisfied passenger. It was an outstanding example of a Moment of Magic.

The passenger was starting in San Francisco. He was going to take a connection to Los Angeles, and then fly to the Orient. Due to weather problems, the flight was delayed. The passenger was upset because he wanted to make his connection to the Orient flight. The Skywest agent phoned another airline, and asked if the passenger could get on that airline's Los Angeles flight.

He was accepted and made a dash to the gate. Once he got there, though, he found out that flight was also delayed. So he dashed back to Skywest and took its flight. If everything went well, he would have just minutes to catch his connecting flight.

Now, the Skywest agent could have stopped there and done nothing more. But he knew the Los Angeles airport, and knew the gate for the customer's connecting flight to the Orient would be way on the other side of the airport from the Skywest gate. So the agent phoned Los Angeles and made arrangements for a Skywest representative to meet the passenger at the gate when he arrived. The Skywest representative in Los Angeles took the passenger in an electric cart to the connecting flight's gate. The flight to the Orient had been notified that this passenger would be arriving, but it would still be a very tight connection for him to make.

The passenger made the connection just in time, and was very grateful to Skywest for its help. By just making a few simple phone calls, the Skywest agent in San Francisco turned a Moment of Misery into a Moment of Magic. This story proves that going the extra mile does not necessarily mean a lot of extra effort or expense. It just requires caring and thinking about the needs of your customer.

By the way, Skywest is bucking the current industry trends by receiving more positive letters than negative ones!

How You Can Make Magic

A magician isn't supposed to reveal how he does his tricks, but I would like to spend the rest of this book sharing insights into how you can create Moments of Magic with your customers.

Start by bringing out the magic that is in you:

- Make a positive impression
- Know your business
- Be informed: know a little about everything
- Show enthusiasm
- Understand your customer

Then, add these ingredients of a Moment of Magic:

- Provide quality
- Respond quickly
- Solve problems and answer needs
- Be reliable
- Say "thank you" and tell your customers they are important

Remember, no matter who you are or what you do, you have customers. Your job and livelihood depend on satisfying the customer. You are your own customer service department.

Whether your customers are high-powered executives, retail shoppers, the employees in the next department or the people in your family, you can build their goodwill and trust...by making Moments of Magic.

Magic Hints!

Be sure to share these tips with your colleagues and others you know.

- The function of every business is to get and keep customers.
- There are two types of customers: external and internal.
- The external customer is the buyer of your product or service.
- Internal customers are the other people with whom you work in your organization.
- Whether or not you deal directly with the external customer, you are involved in customer service.
- Directly or indirectly, everyone serves the outside customer.
- Any time a customer comes into contact with any aspect of your business is a moment of truth.
- A Moment of Magic happens when you have delivered above average service to the customer.
- Everyone is involved in service. You might be a CEO or a bus driver. It doesn't matter. You serve someone.
- Your enterprise is flirting with disaster if you think the customer service department is the only area involved in customer service.

The following link will lead you to more magic hints including articles, videos, and tips:

www.MomentsOfMagicBook.com/chapter1

Or Scan:

"Always do right.
This will surprise some people
and astonish the rest."

—Mark Twain

PART I

What It Takes To Make Magic

Giving outstanding customer service and creating Moments of Magic begins with you! Before you meet your first customer, there are things you need to do to prepare. It is like having important visitors to your house for dinner. You think about the occasion and what will be happening at various times throughout the evening. You get the table set and start to prepare the meal.

Creating magic does not come without effort. You must study and prepare. What you bring to each moment of truth with the customer will have a significant impact on its outcome. Your attitude, appearance, and knowledge are all important. Good business people know how to present themselves, especially in selling situations. Any situation where we service the customer carries some degree of selling. We never stop selling ourselves and our businesses. We must always look for opportunities to highlight our positive attributes and build confidence with our customers. Every server, every bellhop, every cashier, every secretary, every consultant, every accountant, every executive, anyone who contacts the customer – all have a moment of truth and a chance to sell the customer. When you sell the customer and gain their confidence and trust, you have created a Moment of Magic.

So let's wave the magic wand, find out how to harness your positive assets and start making magic!

CHAPTER 2

Make a Positive Impression

"Customers don't distinguish between you and the
company you work for. To the customer's way of
thinking, you are the company."

—Ron Zemke
Author, *Service America*

Someone once said you never get a second chance to make a
first impression. In fact, the opposite is true. We never stop
making first impressions.

Making a good impression yesterday does not mean you do
not have to make a good impression today. It's like the old saying,
"What have you done for me lately?" Every time you are in front
of your customer, you have an opportunity to make an impression.
Every day, you have an opportunity to make a first impression. Remember, this applies not only to the outside customer, but also to
your internal customer, your fellow employees.

The importance of first impressions is illustrated by this true
story from one of the 20th century's truly great communicators,

Bishop Fulton Sheen. He was visiting Philadelphia to give a sermon and decided to walk to the town hall rather than ride. He left the hotel and began walking. Soon, he realized he was lost. He looked around and saw a couple of boys on a playground. He asked one of the boys to come over and told him, "I think I am lost. Can you tell me how to get to the town hall?" The boy said, "Sure, that's easy." He gave directions, and the bishop thanked him.

The bishop asked, "Would you like to come and hear me talk?"

The boy replied, "What are you going to talk about?"

The bishop said, "I am going to talk about how to get to heaven."

The boy stated, "I don't want to hear you talk," and the bishop asked him why.

The boy replied, "You can't figure out how to get to the town hall. I don't see how you can show me how to get to heaven."

The bishop obviously made a negative first impression. That first impression is very important. But even after you've made your first impression, you never stop making impressions. You must keep up the effort every day.

BE UP

When we meet our co-workers, customers, families and other people, we create a first impression of the day. If you walk into the office in the morning cheerful and happy, people will reciprocate and they will treat you nicely. If you walk into the office crabby or withdrawn, you will turn people away. They will not want to talk to you. It is especially important for supervisors to set an air of comfort. Employees need to feel comfortable going to the boss with a problem. Some supervisors carry such a gruff manner that their employees are terrified to bring up any issues.

When you pick up the telephone or greet your customer in person, even if it is the 100th time you've talked to that customer, you create a first impression of the day. You can change and influence your destiny every day in a positive direction or a negative direction. Always be upbeat. Create that Moment of Magic.

Sometimes we are going through difficult personal situations, like illnesses or family crises. It can be difficult not to bring these problems to work, but don't wear them on your sleeves. Keep them to yourself. A professional work environment is not a place to air your personal problems.

In motivating yourself to give your best every day, keep in mind this verse:

> **I shall pass through this world but once.**
> **Any good that I can do,**
> **Or any kindness that I can show,**
> **Let me not defer nor neglect it.**
> **For I shall not pass this way again.**

DRESS AND THE FIRST IMPRESSION

How you look and how you dress are very important. If you are an accountant or an attorney, do you wear the right type of suit? If you work in a restaurant, how do you look? Are your hands clean? Hair combed?

Dressing for success is a topic a lot of people overlook. Don't be one of them! Consider picking up a book on dressing for success. There are many to choose from at your local bookstores and libraries.

Keep in mind that dressing for success does not always mean wearing a suit. It means dressing appropriately for the occasion. Dressing for success may mean one thing in the formal atmosphere of an executive board meeting, but it may mean something entirely different in my office, which is casual.

Often in my office, we are doing physical labor such as putting together manuals for a seminar. It would be silly to wear a business suit on those days.

When it is time for me to do a speech, it is time to dress for success. Then it's time to wear a good suit!

More important than just dressing for success is dressing appropriately. Once I was speaking to a group of installation managers for sprinkler systems. At their meeting, they were dressed casually. In that case, a sport coat, open-collar shirt and a nice pair of slacks were absolutely proper. I knew this audience and I knew that to dress up would turn them off.

Another situation where appropriate did not mean coat and tie was an outdoor speech I did on a summer morning. The temperature was about 96 degrees. My speech was on teamwork, how people can work with one another and do their part to contribute to each other's success. When I arrived at the site, I assessed the situation. I decided to wear my jacket when I was introduced, then immediately take it off.

I wanted to make a good impression by wearing the jacket. I am a professional, and I want to look the part. Then, I wanted to maintain some degree of comfort and show empathy with the heat I knew my audience was feeling. And yes, I was feeling it, too!

OTHER FACTORS

How we maintain our workspaces makes a first impression as well. If you walk into an office that is piled with stacks of papers heaped on top of one another, how can you have confidence this person is going to be able to find information for you?

We form impressions every day among the people we serve and the people we work with. Part of the equation on how well we succeed depends on our attitude and our appearance.

Magic Hints!

Don't forget to share these with the people you work with.

- Every day we create an impression of ourselves for our customers.
- Remember, it is always important to present ourselves at our best.
- Be "up." When you are cheerful, people will reciprocate. Do not let outside problems affect you.
- Dress well. Dress appropriately for the occasion.
- Keep your office space attractive and well organized.
- We never stop making first impressions.

The following link will lead you to more magic hints including articles, videos, and tips:

www.MomentsOfMagicBook.com/chapter2

Or Scan:

CHAPTER 3

Know Your Business

"All wish to possess knowledge, but few, comparatively speaking, are willing to pay the price."

—Juvenal

I f you want to interact effectively with your customers, you must know your business. You must know your product. You must be able to answer questions.

The more you know about your business, the more adept you will be at finding solutions to your customers' needs.

Energizer Battery maintains a close relationship with retail stores. The company positions itself as an expert in retail battery sales and point of purchase displays. It offers to arrange a store's entire battery display, and this includes the competitions' displays. It provides market information on what is selling and what is not.

More importantly, it acts as a source of information on all aspects of the battery market. It is the "category manager." Retailers can go to Energizer with any questions about any aspect of selling batteries and also get good advice on how best to set up their stores.

Pro Plan, a premium pet food brand, provides similar expertise. It positions itself as an expert in space management for the purposes of display and promotion of all pet food items. Pro Plan also provides toll-free 800 telephone service for retailers and customers to call with general questions about pet foods.

A pediatrician I know offers a unique service to parents. He sets aside one hour a day, 8 to 9 a.m., to answer calls from parents. These are not medical emergencies like sick children, just general questions about care and prevention. His patients know this is always a time when he will be available to answer questions.

Become an Expert in Your Field

Knowledge of your own business is vitally important. We never stop learning. We must continually read and study to keep abreast of new developments. When you become an expert in your field, you will gain the respect of your customers, both on the outside and within your organization. You will be looked upon as a source for information.

Why are consultants constantly writing articles, posting blogs and giving seminars? They want to share their expertise and position themselves as experts.

Present yourself as an expert and offer to be a source of information. Customers will come to respect you and will be more likely to come to you for business.

Knowledge Helps Solve Customer Problems

Invest in your own continuing education. The more you know about your business, the better you will be able to solve problems for your customers.

I made a phone call to a prospective client and talked about his needs and interests. He had a current need for a speaker, but I knew I was the wrong person for the job. Sometimes, it's hard to admit that to a client who is ready to sign a contract. But, instead of accepting a job that would have been wrong for the client or saying, "No, I can't help you," I went a step further. I offered to find a speaker who would meet his needs. Part of my business, after all, is knowing my peers and their specialties. I gave the client three names, and one of them got the job.

Did I give up a chance to get business? No. I presented myself as someone who is helpful and knowledgeable. Next time they need a speaker, it is likely they will consider me or at least ask for another referral. I will make myself available to them. I will follow up. I will keep trying until I get the business for myself. Until that time, I will prove to be a valuable resource to them.

KNOW YOUR PRODUCT

You visit a fine restaurant. You study the menu and try to decide what to order. A good server will help you make your choice. The server will explain how different items are prepared and whether the food is spicy or mild. You can ask which items are best, and the server will give recommendations. Contrast this standard with the Moment of Misery I experienced when I asked a server which menu items she would recommend and she replied, "I don't know. I just started working here." Clearly, she hadn't been trained properly before starting the job!

One person who really knows his business is my stockbroker, Jeff Silverstone of Wells Fargo Advisors. I can call him anytime with questions about investments, and he will share his knowledge.

In the beginning, I did not do all my investing business with Jeff. Even if it was an investment I handled through another broker, Jeff was happy to take my call and offer his opinion. He was always glad to help…which is why he now gets all of my business.

Good salespeople must know their businesses, too. If you're going to buy a home or a car, you want to deal with people who can give you solid information. What features come with which price option? What are the estimated utility bills and fuel costs? What does the warranty cover? Technical products such as computers and cell phones, which constantly come out in new models with new features, are an area where most of us are vulnerable. We rely on the salesperson to explain the features of the various products and to help us select which one is right for us. Finding a good salesperson is especially important.

One day I was lucky to meet John Bullock, a salesperson at Neiman Marcus, the upscale department store. John isn't there anymore, but I'll never forget my experience with him. He started out working in the gift department of Neiman Marcus. Out of sheer interest in his work, he began studying about fine china. He went to the library and did research. He became familiar with the stories behind the major names in china such as Wedgwood. Eventually, customers went to him for expert advice and information on china. I don't know what he's doing now, but I suspect that, whatever it is, he's an expert at it!

Read Avidly

How can you become an expert? Noted speaker Brian Tracy says if you read about a subject for an hour each day, within two to three years you will become an expert. If you continue to read about this subject for an hour a day over three to five years, you will become an authority. After five to seven years, you will be an international authority. He adds that if you read just one book a month, you will join the top one percent of the population.

I read every day on subjects related to my business, whether online, with a reading device, or via books or magazines. My reading includes magazines about speaking techniques and about the subjects I cover, such as customer service. I attend seminars and conventions for speakers. I keep abreast of my clients' industries, too.

To better myself in my ability to get clients, I read a magazine called *Personal Selling Power* as well as numerous books on selling and client relations. I also read general publications such as *Communication Briefings, The Wall Street Journal, Bottom Line,* and *Boardroom Reports.*

Read every chance you get, whether it's a physical book or something you enjoy on a special reader like a Kindle. If you have downtime while waiting at the airport or waiting between appointments, that's a good time to read. Check out the nearest newsstand, or bookstore, or public library. Look for books and periodicals outside of your usual reading areas.

Read for fun, too. While most of my reading is business related, I do read fiction. Reading fiction stimulates the imaginative side of the brain, the right brain. It can help us be more creative in solving our everyday problems.

Harvard studies indicate that the key to self-motivation is perpetual growth. Unfortunately, studies also show that 58 percent of American college students never read a nonfiction book after graduation.

No time to read? Try audio books. The average person spends 500 to 1,000 hours a year driving an automobile. What a resource of time to listen and learn! Many popular books, fiction and nonfiction, are available on CD and as audio downloads. If you started to use those 500 to 1,000 hours in your car as learning time, in one year you would gain the learning equal to more than one full semester of college!

DON'T FAKE IT

I assigned an employee to watch a video. I asked her if she had watched it yet, and she said "yes." I asked her opinion, and she gave an evasive answer.

The next day she came into my office and said, "I feel like an idiot. I should have just told you I didn't watch the video."

I thanked her for her honesty. Knowing your business is great, but if the topic gets past what you know, don't try to fake it. Sooner or later, it will backfire on you.

A number of years ago, freshmen members entering Congress fell victim to a prank that tested their knowledge of world events.

A reporter called 20 incoming congressmen and asked, "Do you think we're doing enough to stop ethnic cleansing in Freedonia?" At the time, ethnic cleansing was a serious issue in the former Yugoslavian territory of Bosnia. The incoming members of Congress should probably have known that Freedonia was a fictitious country, even if they didn't know it was from the Marx Brothers movie *Duck Soup*.

All the congressmen fell for the prank! They gave answers like, "I think anything we can do to use the good offices of the U.S. government to assist stopping the killing over there, we should do." None of the freshmen congressmen thought to ask further about Freedonia, like where it was or who had made the reports of ethnic cleansing. They gave answers that seemed to be politically correct... even though the only way they could conceivably have heard of Freedonia was as a gag thought up by Groucho Marx!

Magic Hints!

These are great tips to share through social media.

- Knowing your business makes you better able to help your customers.
- Become an expert in your field. Build a reputation as the person to call for information about your area of business.
- Know your product and all its features.
- Read avidly. Read professional magazines, business periodicals and fiction. Attend seminars.
- Listen to audio books in your car.
- Using the 500 to 1,000 annual hours in your car as audio learning time = at least one full semester of college!
- The more you know about your business, the better you will be able to solve problems for your customers.

The following link will lead you to more magic hints including articles, videos, and tips:

www.MomentsOfMagicBook.com/chapter3

Or Scan:

CHAPTER 4

Be Informed:
Know A Little About A Lot

"If a man empties his purse into his head, no one can take it away from him. An investment in knowledge always pays the best interest."

—Benjamin Franklin

What if you were invited to have dinner this evening with the presidents of the five largest companies in America, or if you found yourself sitting next to an interesting person on an airplane? Could you hold your own in conversation? You can make a positive impression by demonstrating you are a well-rounded individual. Show that you have knowledge and interests not only in your specific field, but also the world as a whole. You don't have to be an expert. You just need to know enough to have some sense of what is going on.

General knowledge is knowing a little about a lot of things. It is knowing about world events and about the arts and sports. General knowledge is gained by reading the paper or watching the news. A great paper to read is *USA Today*. The articles are short and to the point. A great television program to watch is *60 Minutes* or one of the other good feature news shows. An interesting magazine that has great human interest stories is *People*. You will be surprised what you can pick up by just spending a few minutes reading the front page of each section of your local paper or a website like Google News. The great thing about Google News is that it lets you customize your news page with specific keywords, so you can stay up-to-date on any topic you choose and create the "newspaper" that is perfect for you. A site like the *Huffington Post* (www.huffpost.com) not only lets you set up the news topics you like, but also lets you comment and share to your heart's content! That's not a small thing, because the more engaged you are with a topic, the more likely you are to learn about it. If you learn a little about a lot of things, when you get in front of your customers you can talk about things other than business. You can find out what their hobbies are and the things they like to do. Ask questions about what they do and discuss the answers. They will appreciate and respect your interest in them.

General knowledge helps to build rapport with customers. Aside from becoming an expert at what you do, you need to know what is going on in the world on a daily basis. If someone asks your opinion on a current issue, you should have something to say.

Not knowing about current events could make a negative impression. What if your customers are talking about a certain actor or hit movie that you don't know about, or even more importantly, a major news event? It could put you in an awkward situation.

In my profession as a speaker, it is expected that I have some knowledge of current events and trends. Other fields where this is important are marketing, advertising and public relations. For a barber or a bartender, the best reason to know current events is to be able to converse with customers. Even if you do not come into contact with the company's customers, you still work with people, your inside customers, every day.

Keep up with current events. You will build stronger and more interesting relationships with your customers and the people with whom you work.

Magic Hints!

- General knowledge of the world shows you are a well-rounded individual.
- Learn a little about everything. Know enough about current events, art and sports to keep up a conversation.
- Knowledge contributes to building better relationships with your customers and people with whom you work.
- Know enough to have some sense of what is going on outside of your field of expertise.
- The more you know about your business, the better you will be able to solve problems for your customers.

The following link will lead you to more magic hints including articles, videos, and tips:

www.MomentsOfMagicBook.com/chapter4

Or Scan:

CHAPTER 5

Be Enthusiastic

"There is nothing as powerful and contagious as
positive, uplifting enthusiasm that is handled
wisely by a group of people who love one another
and contribute their individual talents and abili-
ties, coming together as one united force to reach
one common cause, goal or dream."

—Carl Mays

I f you are not excited about what you do or what you sell, how
are you going to get another person excited? Enthusiasm is
contagious. If you are excited, it will cause other people to
become excited. Enthusiastic people are fun to be around.

It can work the other way, too. If you are not excited, then they
are not going to be excited either. Famous speaker Danny Cox says,

**"Enthusiasm is contagious. If what you have is
lack of enthusiasm, that is also contagious."**

Just one's tone of voice makes a big difference. Speaking in

an energetic and enthusiastic tone of voice will spark enthusiasm in others.

Being excited about something lends credibility to what you do
or sell. The person must really be involved in what is going on and
believe in what he or she is saying.

When we are alone, we can work extremely hard and be very serious. But when somebody walks into the office, or any time we meet
the public, we must show enthusiasm. If you have just finished a
project, it might be appropriate to show some excitement and enthusiasm. That could impact the results your project eventually achieves.

GIVE 100 PERCENT

All of us go through energy cycles. Sometimes we are enthusiastic.
Sometimes we are flat. The trick is to overcome those tired, lackluster times. Do not let your customer see any difference. Put your
best foot forward every day, no matter what may have happened to
you the night before.

I once did a program for a client when I was feeling absolutely
miserable. I was sick. In fact, I was so sick that I was rushed to the
hospital the night after the program with a 105-degree temperature.

Fortunately, in spite of my being sick, I did get a good reaction
to the speech. I put forth a 100 percent effort and didn't complain
about the way I felt. The proof that this was the right approach was
that I booked four more engagements with the same client.

For another company, I had contracted to do a series of 12
speeches in a three-week period. On the last leg of this tour, I became ill. By now, I had become very comfortable with my speech
material and I knew exactly what the audience wanted.

I stayed in bed in my hotel room until it was almost time to
go on. Then, I woke myself up and took a really quick shower. I
went out there and put everything I had into that presentation.
Five minutes after the speech, I was back in bed. Not one person in
that audience ever knew I was sick.

Being enthusiastic means rising to the occasion and giving 100 percent of your effort. Former professional racquetball player Doug Cohen knows what it means to give 100 percent. Whether on pro tour, in tournaments or just practicing, he always gave 100 percent. On days when he woke up tired, he would still get up and play. At times when most players would quit practicing because of fatigue or boredom, he would continue at the same pace, if not harder. This type of practice paid off when he was tired in the middle of an important match. He had disciplined himself to continue his 100 percent effort...even when he was down or tired.

This philosophy has carried over into Doug's career as a real estate professional. All of Doug's clients know and appreciate the effort and dedication he puts in for them.

Your customers will not accept "I don't feel good" as an excuse for poor service. Having a rough night or not having a day off in a week or having sick children are not acceptable excuses for a poor attitude on the job.

HAVE A POSITIVE ATTITUDE

Maintaining a positive attitude is important in order to show enthusiasm.

Do not let your problems drag you down. Avoid feeling sorry for yourself. Do not fuss over things you can't change.

Instead, look at your assets. Focus on what you can affect. Set goals and work to achieve them.

In your everyday life, find good things to say about yourself and others. Set out to make each day a great day. Live each moment for the best. Motivational speaker Dennis Waitley asks,

> **"Do we sing because we are happy? Or are we happy because we sing?"**

No one likes to be around people who are always negative and complaining. There is a man at my health club who is a chronic whiner. He makes up names for people. Instead of calling me Shep, he whines, "Oh, Shepola." He never smiles.

I've never seen him laugh. He doesn't seem to have any major problems in his life; he has a nice family, even a dog. But I would never want to be around him outside of the health club. He would just bring me down.

Problems create opportunities. Whenever anything negative has happened in my life, I have always said, "There is a reason for this." Whenever I have an extremely negative thing happen to me, I realize that there are people out there who have it a lot worse. Children lose their parents, parents lose their children. Disease takes over someone's body. Compared to them, my problems are unimportant.

Even if you do not have control over the problem, the one thing you always have control over is your attitude. Your choices are what make it a great day or a lousy day.

I once was driving around New Orleans with a client. We were looking for the restaurant where his customers were meeting us for dinner, and we got lost and ended up in a bad neighborhood. We were turning on this street and that street and had no idea where we were. The neighborhoods were getting worse. Our tension and apprehension were building. My client was really starting to get upset. So I made a joke. I sarcastically said, "Oh boy, I'm going to die in New Orleans."

My client laughed. He then asked, "Okay, where are we?"

I said, "I know exactly where we are. We're right here. I don't know exactly where we're going, but we're making good time."

My client started to feel better as we made some levity out of the situation. And, obviously, we did survive. We were a few minutes late to dinner. We could have been angry or upset about it, but our attitudes kept us in good spirits.

LOW-KEY PEOPLE CAN BE ENTHUSIASTIC

You do not always have to be an exciting, dynamic person to have enthusiasm. Everyone is different in how they express themselves.

No matter who you are, you do have enthusiasm and can project it.

Your enthusiasm shows in the passion you have for your work. My former business associate Paul Wirtz is a perfect example of a low-key type of individual who still captivates you with his enthusiasm. We did a lot of work together training people to become expense reduction consultants. Paul has been in this business for many years, and he knows it inside and out.

Whenever we presented together, there was always big contrast between Paul and me. I am a very energetic and expressive speaker, whereas Paul's presentation style is completely opposite of mine. Paul was (and is) an accountant by training, so he is very laid back and somewhat detail-oriented. I used to joke about how when Paul was younger, he had a charisma bypass. Yet he would keep his audiences on the edge of their seats as much as I did. That is because he always showed passion about his life's work and that passion always showed through. He brought a dynamic energy from within, which had nothing to do with jumping around on a platform, getting people excited, or making people laugh. He did it all through his credibility and his desire to do a good job.

Have you ever noticed this in someone? Often the president of a large corporation may be a terrible public speaker, but his employees and stockholders still respond positively to him. Why? Because he is knowledgeable and respected. If you believe in yourself and your own life experience, your credibility will show through. Your passion radiates energy and enthusiasm, even though it may not be physical energy, but mental energy.

KNOWLEDGE AND INVOLVEMENT BUILD ENTHUSIASM

Use your company's product, read about your subject, and get involved in your field. That is one reason why an automobile salesperson drives his or her demonstrator vehicle home.

If you sell home and personal care products, use them yourself.

If you sell computers, use what you sell and read the personal computing magazines and websites.

You also can build enthusiasm by getting involved in your profession. Join professional groups. Volunteer for committees and projects. Meet and talk with your peers. Attending a workshop or meeting not only educates you, but it also can also give you a fresh charge of energy.

Magic Hints!

- Always show enthusiasm for what you do. Enthusiasm adds credibility.
- Give 100 percent – even when you feel lackluster.
- Have a positive attitude. See the positives in every situation. Don't fuss over things you cannot change.
- Low-key people show enthusiasm by their sincerity and passion.
- To build your enthusiasm, use your company's product, read about your subject and get more involved.
- If you believe in yourself and your own life experience, your credibility will show through.

The following link will lead you to more magic hints including articles, videos, and tips:

www.MomentsOfMagicBook.com/chapter5

Or Scan:

CHAPTER 6

Understand Your Customer

**"If we are not customer driven,
our cars won't be either."**

**—Donald Peterson
Former CEO,
Ford Motor Company**

W ho are your customers? What are their needs and wants? Businesses spend millions on market research to learn about their customers. They study demographics and lifestyles. They test market products before investing in a full rollout.

As you work to build relationships with your customers, these are some of the most important words to remember:

Think like the buyer, not like the supplier.

A buzzword in many fields today is *market-driven*. What that means is that an organization is developing its products or programs based on needs it has identified with its customers. It is thinking like the buyer.

The opposite of being market-driven is being sales-driven. A sales-driven organization says, "We have a warehouse full of widgets. We must find people to buy our widgets. Advertise, repackage, do whatever we have to do, but please, sell those widgets." For years, companies have gotten away with that philosophy. But it just will not work in the competitive marketplace of the present day.

It has been said that in the 1950s and 1960s, Americans had lower expectations of products. When they bought new cars, they expected defects and tolerated them. They were not upset when windows wouldn't open or the car's tires were under-inflated. Then the Japanese came along with zero-defect cars. Americans now carry higher expectations of cars and other products they buy. Our U.S. auto manufacturers are working hard to increase their quality, and they have become very competitive!

BE SENSITIVE TO CUSTOMER NEEDS

Put yourself in your customers' shoes. Consider how you would behave or react if you were in their situation.

Nintendo, for instance, really understands the people who buy its video games. The company knows that its customers, mostly young people, quickly master the games and become bored with them. They have a steady appetite for new games, but there also is a concern that if players get stuck or frustrated with the games, they may shelve their Nintendo sets and find other entertainment. So Nintendo has a team of hundreds of game counselors answering telephone and on-line inquiries from the company headquarters in Redmond, Washington.

Service hours are 4 a.m. to midnight, Pacific Time, Monday through Saturday, with shorter hours on Sunday. This is convenient for all time zones (when it's 4 a.m. in Seattle, it's 7 a.m. in New York) and for the evening times when kids are playing the games. How many 10-year-olds would be allowed to make a long distance call during business hours from school?

Here's a true story about Nintendo's concern for the customer. Back in 2007, a Nintendo customer in Redmond, Washington, broke her Wii after a marathon session of Wii Sports with her six-year-old son. She called Nintendo customer care, having found the support number on the company's website. (Not every company these days likes to promote the call-in number on the Internet!) She got the customer service person on the phone and explained the situation. The Nintendo rep said, "Oh, you live in Washington? Bring it on over to Nintendo headquarters, then. We'll fix it right up." And they did!

FedEx/Kinko's Copies is another great example of a company that's structured around consumer needs. Its primary markets are self-employed people, homemakers and college students. Following through on its initial brand commitment of serving as "your branch office," FedEx/Kinko's strives to be a one-stop shop for all copying, document and package delivery services. Open 24 hours a day, a typical store has standard copiers, oversize copiers, color copiers, fax machines and a bank of Internet-connected PC and Mac computers available to customers. Sitting next to the copiers are supplies of scissors, tape, white-out and other items a customer might need to make final adjustments to a document. FedEx/Kinko's Copies is ready for customers and caters exactly to what they need.

Ask Your Customers

Make an effort to find out what your customers' needs are. Solicit their comments. Cavett Robert, the founder of the National Speakers Association, tells a story about a boy visiting a soda shop. He orders a root beer float, and while it is being made he goes over to the pay phone. The man behind the counter is listening in. The boy says, "Hello, Ma'am, I was calling to see if you need your grass cut today. Oh, you already have someone doing your grass? Does he edge around the sidewalk? Does he sweep up? Okay. So you're happy with the service? Thank you anyway." He hangs up the phone.

The man behind the counter says, "I heard your conversation, and I'm sorry."

The boy asks, "Sorry about what?"

The man says, "It's obvious you didn't get the job."

The boy replies, "Oh, don't worry. There is nothing to be sorry about. I'm the one who already has the job. I was just calling to make sure I'm doing a good job."

This is what it takes. We have to stay in touch with our customers. We have to ask if they are happy, and we have to ask what we can do to improve.

We want our customers to be demanding. We want them to bring their opinions to us. As long as they do that and we do our jobs, the customer will keep coming back. When the competition gets fierce, they will stay with us regardless of price. They will stay when they know we are giving them something they cannot get anywhere else.

The importance of asking the customer was a lesson learned the hard way for a hotel and conference center on the West Coast. Looking to increase its convention business, it had produced a beautiful brochure filled with colorful pictures of all of the center's amenities: golf, tennis, swimming and exercise facilities. The brochure was a huge failure. Why? Because the hotel did not ask the customers what they were looking for. The hotel did not think like the buyer. The buyers of this hotel's convention services are meeting planners who schedule large group events. From a meeting planner's standpoint, amenities like golf and tennis are a secondary issue. The planner has other concerns: How big are the meeting rooms? How are they configured? What audio visual services are available? If those questions are answered satisfactorily, *then* the planner becomes interested in the amenities.

After learning from its mistake, this hotel asked its customers about their needs before it launched into expensive advertising campaigns. It held focus groups and surveyed the customers. It now does this in many areas of its business. One survey on coffee breaks produced an interesting result. Before the survey, the catering department predicted what seemed to be obvious: that coffee, tea and Danish are the most important part of coffee breaks. Guess what? They were wrong. Do you know what the meeting planners considered the most important part of coffee breaks? Bathrooms. Meeting planners want to know how many bathrooms there are and how close they are to the meeting room. Executives in a meeting, after sitting for two or three hours, need to use the bathroom. They do not want to wait in line. The next priority is telephones. While on break, they want to call the office. There need to be enough telephones so the important executives do not have to wait to make their calls, and, more importantly, are not late for the next meeting. Incidentally, coffee was at the bottom of the list, the least important part of a coffee break.

This is a good example of how it pays to think like the buyer, not like the supplier. Formal surveys, or website-driven questionnaires like those at SurveyMonkey.com, are just one way to find out what your customer is thinking. Small focus groups can give you great feedback. You can also use informal sampling techniques, like making a few calls to a random selection of prospects in the field or asking questions and chatting with your customers while you do other business. Some of my best feedback comes by sitting next to my clients on an airplane while returning from a speaking engagement.

One way that Anheuser-Busch finds out what its customers think is by sending its executives into the field. The formal name for the program is "All Aboard." Executives will go out with delivery drivers in their trucks and ride to the various stops including grocery stores, liquor stores, restaurants and taverns. The executives will hear directly from retailers what their concerns are and what are those of their customers. The executives get a firsthand view of the market. This has to be one of the reasons Anheuser-Busch is number one.

Another good technique is comment cards. Wherever I go, I always fill out the comment cards. Typically, a comment card will ask the customer to rate various aspects of the company's product or service. There is one question that is more effective than any other on a comment card. It should be the first one asked on the card. I call it the "One Thing" question. Here it is:

What one thing can you think of that could have made this experience better?

If customers are mentioning the same issue over and over, then you know this is an area where you need to pay attention. The beauty of this kind of survey is that it is open-ended and unprompted. You have not limited the customer's response by asking closed-ended or multiple choice questions. Problem areas can be brought to your attention.

USE YOUR IMAGINATION

Once you have found out what your customers think and need, develop creative solutions to meet those needs.

Always ask, "How can we serve you better?" If more and more of your customers come from a certain area, perhaps you should open a branch office in that vicinity. If most of your customers are working people, perhaps you should establish evening hours.

Do you remember the movie *Big*? In it, Tom Hanks plays a boy who gets trapped in the body of a young man in his 20s. He gets a job at a toy company. The owner of the toy company spots him playing with some of the toys. Hanks offers some radical ideas for changing the toys which prove to be an immense success. This is because they come from the mind of a 10-year-old who happens to be occupying an adult body. Hanks' best friend, still 10 years old, comes to visit him at the office and sees him playing with toys. "Don't you work?" he asks.

Hanks replies, "Working? I just play with these toys and tell them what I think. They pay me to play with toys!"

Creativity is seeing things from different directions. Professional speaker Joel Weldon says there are five ways to be creative:

- Combination: Putting together two dissimilar items
- Adaptation: Taking an idea from somewhere else and applying it
- Substitution: Putting a different item in place of another
- Minification: Making an object smaller
- Magnification: Making an object larger

Joel uses the tape recorder as an example to illustrate this. Combination would be replacing a tape recorder and radio with one unit that has both. A child's toy tape recorder is adaptation. Substitution occurred when built-in microphones replaced separate hand-held mikes. Minification was the "Walkman," followed by the MP3 player, followed by the iPod; magnification was the "boom box."

There is a great book titled *If It Ain't Broke, Break It* by Robert Kriegel and Louis Patler. Break it thinking is a good approach. We need to keep questioning and challenging. "But we've always done it that way" is not an acceptable answer.

Back in the 1970s, Japanese carmakers began providing one key to fit both the ignition and car doors. Although research showed that customers preferred one key, it took some U.S. car companies 15 years to figure out that a single key was what consumers wanted.

We must constantly change the rules and assumptions we live by in the face of changing customer needs. Service is not just being nice and patting customers on the back, it is giving them quality at every turn. It is giving them the product they want, and if it does not meet their needs, making it meet their needs. It means changing it as necessary. As the world progresses and people grow, consumers and their needs change. Giving excellent service encompasses meeting and anticipating the customer's expectations at every turn and understanding your customer.

Magic Hints!

- Put yourself in your customer's shoes.
- Be sensitive to customer needs. Understand when and how customers use your product or service.
- Ask your customers for their opinions. Conduct formal surveys (including online surveys) and use customer comment cards. Survey customers informally as you talk with them in person or by phone.
- The most important question on a customer comment card is, "Is there any one thing that we can do to serve you better?"
- Use your imagination to develop creative solutions to meet your customers' needs.
- Think like the buyer, not the supplier.

The following link will lead you to more magic hints including articles, videos, and tips:

www.MomentsOfMagicBook.com/chapter6

Or Scan:

−Be our guest,
Be our guest,
Put our service to the test,
Tie your napkin round your neck, cherie
And we'll provide the rest…
Why, we only live to serve.

—From the Walt Disney soundtrack
"Beauty and the Beast" by Howard Ashman and
Alan Menken

PART II

Ways to Create Moments of Magic

Y ou have decided to become a Magic Maker with your customers. You have polished your first impression and developed your knowledge about your business and the world around you. You are charged up and enthusiastic, and you have learned all about your customers' needs and desires. You want to stand out from the crowd and do what it takes to get and keep that customer. Customers today have high expectations. There is a lot of competition. You cannot get away with delivering a shoddy product or poor service. Following are five ways to set yourself apart with Moments of Magic.

CHAPTER 7

Provide Quality At Every Turn

"Quality is not an act, it is a habit."

—Aristotle

Webster's defines quality as "excellence, superiority." Customers today want and demand quality. Shoddy products quickly gain poor reputations and fall by the wayside. Witness the Yugo automobile, which became the brunt of comedians' jokes because of poor reliability and eventual pull-out of the U.S. market. Yugo's failure also shows that customers do not make decisions on price alone. They will not buy a cheap product if it does not have acceptable quality.

Shoddy service leaves a company or organization with a poor reputation. If you go to a restaurant and have a bad experience, would you tell your friends to go there? Would you return to a mechanic who does sloppy work on your car if you had any other option?

In today's marketplace, you need a good product and good service to succeed. That is called providing quality at every turn.

People expect a quality job and a quality product…quality in every aspect of what you do. Quality has become the buzzword as Americans have become educated on issues of quality. Consumerism has taught the public about what it can and should expect from business.

If nothing else, you must be aware of the quality of your competition. You must be at least as good as they are. You can't let the competition beat you on quality. As long as your quality is competitive, you can surpass your competition through good service. Whether you deal directly with the outside customer or your customers are your fellow employees, you need to give your best and put quality into everything you do.

Lexus – An Example of Quality

Since their introduction in the U.S. market in the 1980s, Lexus automobiles have enjoyed phenomenal success. A new brand name created by Toyota to compete in the luxury market, Lexus has taken large numbers of customers from German luxury barons Mercedes and BMW as well as the American stalwart Cadillac. One reason why Lexus has been so successful is its complete dedication to quality at every turn. Here is part of the "Lexus Cares" mission statement:

> **"The challenge before Lexus is to create a new class of high performance and luxury in the automobile market. How will we do it? First we will offer a uniquely intelligent blend of functional technology, engineering and quality craftsmanship in our products. Then, we will complete the luxury experience by providing an unprecedented level of excellence in convenience and personalized attention in customer service."**

Mercedes and BMW have reputations for outstanding engineering. Lexus holds its own with them in engineering, but what really sets Lexus apart from its competition is service.

Here is an example of how Lexus does things differently. A while back, the company had to recall some of its vehicles. Usually, when there is a recall, a company will send form letters to product owners and put a notice in the news media. Did Lexus issue its recall this way? No, because Lexus is not an ordinary car company. Instead, Lexus personally telephoned all the owners of affected Lexus cars. The representative asked when would be a convenient time for the dealer to come pick up the consumer's Lexus from his or her home or business and bring it in for the repair. While the Lexus was being repaired, the customer would receive another Lexus to use. That is service!

You won't find this kind of service from an ordinary company. Lexus' extraordinary attitude about service pervades every aspect of the operation. The following statement, titled "What Is Lexus?" is distributed to the company's dealers and sales force:

**"Lexus is…Engineering sophistication
and manufacturing quality.
Lexus is…Luxury and performance.
Lexus is…An image and expectation of excellence.
Lexus is…Valuing the customer as
an important individual.
Lexus is…Treating customers the way
THEY want to be treated.
Lexus is…A total experience that reflects professionalism and a sincere commitment to satisfaction.
Lexus is…Doing it right the first time.
Lexus is…Caring on a personal level.
Lexus is…Exceeding customer expectations.
And…In the eyes of the customer, I AM LEXUS!!!"**

QUALITY IS SOMETHING THAT LASTS

Quality service means nothing if the product keeps breaking and has to be repaired constantly.

A telephone equipment company once found out what problems poor materials can create. It had outstanding service people, and its phones and switching equipment were well made. However, it compromised on wiring and other peripheral materials. The service people had to keep going back for repeat service calls to the same customers. No matter how good the service people were, the system was going to keep breaking. Trained people and a good service philosophy could not make up for poor materials.

Lasting quality applies to more than just automobiles, appliances and other mechanical devices. Those serving internal customers have important quality considerations. Perhaps you have been asked to write a report. Delivering quality is doing a thorough job and making sure the report truly reflects the situation as you know it. The quality report presents the necessary information to make a sound decision.

Those who skimp on quality may do the minimum and "tell them what they want to hear." Others may supply volumes of meaningless information just to give the impression of thoroughness.

For a consultant, quality is asking the tough questions and delving into the deeper issues with a client. Builders and architects achieve quality when they design buildings that meet all foreseeable needs of the people who will use the building. Quality building design is setting standards and tolerances to withstand major earthquakes and other extreme circumstances.

QUALITY IS CLEANLINESS

One day many years ago, Walt Disney took his young daughter to an amusement park. The roller coaster was rickety, and the place generally was dirty.

"How could anyone take a child here?" he asked himself. "One day, I want to create a theme park where families can enjoy themselves, and know it is safe to go there." So Disney bought a plot of orange groves in Anaheim, California. The rest is history. Today, Disney theme parks set a quality standard for the rest of the industry. They are meticulously clean, and personnel are always friendly and hospitable. Disney theme parks show how cleanliness is part of quality.

If you take your car to a repair shop and find the shop filled with grease and a mess of parts and tools, doesn't it make you wonder what they will do with your car? It's an unwritten rule that a good measure of a repair shop is its cleanliness.

Another way to show cleanliness and quality is in your written materials. Quality is cleanly typed correspondence, and clean, attractive literature. Quality is words spelled correctly and sentences well written. If you receive a piece of sales literature that looks like the 12th generation of pieces assembled on a 1990s photocopier, doesn't it make you wonder about the professionalism of the people behind it? With all the capabilities of modern word processing and graphic layout systems (including spell-check and grammar-check) there's no excuse for messy marketing materials.

QUALITY IS VALUE

When we spend our money, we want to feel we are getting our money's worth. If I spend $17,000 on a Nissan Sentra, I expect a reliable, economical, reasonably comfortable car. If I spend $40,000 for a Lexus, I expect all of this at a much higher level. For the price of the Lexus, I am much pickier about ride, handling and amenities like the stereo system. And I expect each car to be at least as good as the competition in its class. For dinner, I can go to an exclusive Italian restaurant in the famed Hill section of St. Louis and have a chicken parmesan dinner for around $80 a person, including drinks and tip. Or, I can get chicken parmesan at a chain restaurant and pay $10 a person. At the expensive restaurant, I expect a high degree of refinement in the cooking, the service and the atmosphere. At the chain restaurant, I expect a good tasting meal delivered quickly and politely in a pleasant atmosphere. In either case, I expect something in line with what I am paying.

Years ago, Toyota differentiated itself from other cars on the basis of quality. It said its doors would slam just as quietly as those on luxury cars. The implication was you could get the same level of quality from a Toyota for much less money than a luxury car. Therefore, the consumer could save money but still receive the high quality usually promised by more expensive brands.

There is a famous delicatessen in New York City called Carnegie's Deli. People pay twice as much for a sandwich there than at most other delicatessens around the country. What do you receive for your money? One, the unique, distinctly New York experience of the place, with the waiters' playful "Don't give me no trouble" attitude. And two, sandwiches that are so thick that you probably won't finish them. They are always filling! You will never leave hungry. Carnegie's is not a sandwich; it is an experience, and that is what the customers are paying for. You get a lot for your money!

QUALITY IS INFORMATION

You can enhance the quality of your product or service by giving information to your customer. People like to know about you and your product. Everyone may not be interested, but for some, information about your products and services can be a Moment of Magic.

When you take something to be repaired, it always helps when the service person explains what the problem is, and why it occurred. If you are having a home built, it is nice to know the grade of the lumber and how far apart the wall studs are being placed. It may be interesting to receive information about the history of the property and the area on which your home is being built.

Information can be given one-on-one by sales or service people, or it can be disseminated through brochures and other written information.

Many national associations in the health care field publish pamphlets for use in doctors' and dentists' offices. Subjects range from orthodontic care to orthopedics.

On the side of every can of Budweiser beer, the label explains the Beechwood Aging process used to brew the beer.

Some businesses, such as consultants and hospitals, publish newsletters for their customers and prospects.

For internal customers, you can regularly prepare reports about your work and circulate these to other key people. Also, try to present your report in person, rather than just toss it in someone's in-basket.

Lack of information can definitely be a negative. Have you ever bought something, and then found you couldn't use it because you could not understand the directions? It went on the shelf. Computer software, hardware, accessories and video games are notorious for poor or incomplete directions and user-hostile design. On the other hand, some products are so well designed and deliver a user experience that is so intuitive, that they pretty much serve as their own instruction manuals. Consider the iPad, which may be the ultimate information tool of our era: tens of millions of people know exactly how to use it...yet it has no printed manual! If you stop to think about it, shouldn't that be the standard of quality for any good information tool?

Information is a tool you can use to sell your customers on you and your product and reinforce the sale again and again. Use it well, and make sure it supports an experience that people want to come back to and experience again!

Magic Hints!

- People expect quality.
- Study your competition and make sure you are at least equal on quality. Beat them with superior service.
- Give lasting value. Provide a durable product. Do it right the first time, every time.
- Quality is cleanliness. Keep your facilities clean. Make your people look good. Make correspondence neat, clean and attractive.
- Give customers their money's worth and more.
- Do not skimp. Be like the restaurant that gives generous portions.
- Provide information. Explain the product and how it is made. Let the customer know what you do, how you do it and why you do it.
- Provide status reports and project updates.
- As long as your quality is competitive, you can exceed your competition through good service.

The following link will lead you to more magic hints including articles, videos, and tips:

www.MomentsOfMagicBook.com/chapter7

Or Scan:

CHAPTER 8

Respond Quickly

**"Of course I want it today. If I wanted it tomorrow,
I would have given it to you tomorrow."**

—The Boss

We live in the age of instant information and instant response. On our cell phones, we can watch wars being fought halfway around the world. Within seconds, we can email business documents to Japan or Poland or Egypt. We keep up with what friends and family are doing and where they are doing it on platforms like Facebook and Twitter. We can walk into a grocery store, pick up a couple of items, walk over to the cashier and watch as he or she scans the items across a little electric eye. We hear a beep, and a moment later, the cashier tells us how much we owe and gives us a coupon for our next visit based on what we bought today.

We are all conditioned for quick response. What used to take minutes or days to calculate now can be done in a matter of seconds, if not instantaneously. So when it comes to people, customers expect the same quick response they are used to getting from today's technology.

More than ever, it is imperative that we handle customer requests on a timely basis. Quick response is important. The speed at which you take care of a customer will greatly enhance the chances of the customer coming back to you again. For internal customers, the speed at which you respond will enhance the confidence that fellow employees have in you to get things done.

Reality check: many of our customers (both internal and external) are now expecting responses from us, not in days, not in hours, but in minutes!

One thing that differentiates some successful people is how fast they work with the client. Some people take weeks or even months to get information back to the client, while others can literally do it in hours or minutes. Ironically, they are giving the same information!

If you come back right away, the client is still excited about the project. If you wait for weeks or months, you could face a response like, "Oh, you're back. I wondered if you ever were coming back." If someone inquired about my business and I did not respond quickly, chances are that client would move on to someone else who did respond quickly.

Once, I almost lost a prospective client because of a lost telephone message. The client called on a Monday morning and explained politely that he needed a speaker, it was the second time he had called, was I interested or not? I did not know about the previous call on Friday, because the message had not been given to me. I asked when he needed the speaker, and he said next week. I reacted quickly. Since the client was located in my hometown of St. Louis, I decided to send an information packet by courier. The client had the material within the hour. That same day, the client received material from two other speakers. Fortunately, I got the job. No doubt, my quick response that Monday morning gained me an edge with this client. Here is the basic rule to follow when it comes to timelines:

Don't keep the customer waiting.

Depending on what you do, the length of time required to respond will vary. If you have a request from someone to send a piece of literature, email it immediately, or if you don't have and can't get an email address, ensure that it is put in that day's postal mail. If you must do some research or prepare a report, the process could take a little longer.

Telephone calls always should be returned the same day. An even better goal is within an hour or two. Whatever you do, avoid the mentality of some company executives who never return phone calls or answer memos. You have to call them five times to get an answer on something. Avoid the attitude of some organizations that publicly announce they need four to six weeks to process simple requests for literature.

Ask When They Want It

Some things really need to be done right away, and some don't. Start by asking your customer when they need what they are requesting. This is especially true for internal customers.

You have to understand people's language. "As soon as possible" may mean today for your boss. It may mean within the month to someone else. Find out what the response time needs to be. If you are given an unrealistic time frame, then tell the person what he or she can realistically expect from you and by when. There may be time needed to conduct research, build sample products or do artwork.

If you cannot respond immediately with a full answer, at least start by acknowledging the request. Write an email message back saying, "We received your request. It will take 'x-time' to process." Then, explain why it will take more time. Another technique is to provide interim reports or executive summaries. Perhaps you have just done a survey. You've tabulated the data and you know what the findings are, but you have not put together the full report. Your executive has an important meeting tomorrow, and there isn't time to finish the final report. What you can do, though, is prepare a memo to the executive summarizing "preliminary findings."

Here is another example. A consultant has been brought in to study a certain area of the client's business. The client is eager to hear the results of the study. The consultant could say, "I cannot give you full information now, since there is a lot of research to do. However, I will give you weekly updates. This is where I am now, and this is the next step. This is when it will be finished." The client normally will understand, provided there are legitimate reasons. You cannot just say, "I didn't get around to it." Delays can and do occur. Those are acceptable, but procrastination is not.

You should bring a sense of urgency to all your dealings with the client. Do not put off until tomorrow what can be done today. Do not keep the customer waiting. Provide a time frame and stick to it.

Magic Hints!

- In this age of information, rapid response is the norm.
- The speed at which you take care of a customer will greatly enhance the chances of the customer coming back again.
- Do not keep the customer waiting.
- Return phone calls and answer emails and letters promptly.
- Ask when the customer needs what he or she is requesting.
- If you cannot fulfill the request immediately, acknowledge the request and provide a timetable. Give status reports.
- Bring a sense of urgency to all your dealings with the client.

The following link will lead you to more magic hints including articles, videos, and tips:

www.MomentsOfMagicBook.com/chapter8

Or Scan:

CHAPTER 9

Solve Their Problems

"Use your own best judgment at all times."

**—The entire policy manual
of Nordstrom's**

S olving problems is the direct action phase of Moments of Magic. This is where you go to work for the customer. You will have the chance to harness your creative talents to find "win-win" solutions to the stickiest of situations.

We face a wide variety of problems. Sometimes, it may be something as simple as "I've moved, please update my address." On the other hand, you may be an attorney who has been asked to negotiate a complex series of deals to protect a client's interest. And some problems are immediate, like a car that will not start.

You can also look at problems in a long-term view. You may look beyond the immediate situation, and think more deeply about the needs of the customer. A local bank was hearing more and more of its customers say they work during the day and could not get to the bank when it was open. The bank's response was to extend its hours into the evening. Don't you wish more banks did that?

Fix the Problem

When the customer gives you a problem, make sure you solve it. The worst thing that can happen is for the customer to have to come back again to get something fixed. That's a big turnoff.

The bottom line is this:

> **You can be knowledgeable and enthusiastic and respond quickly, but if you do not fix the problem, you will not satisfy the customer.**

Here are three steps to help put you on track toward solving problems.

Listen to your customer. Hear the whole story. Don't jump to the conclusion that this is just like another situation you have handled. Ask clarifying questions.

Understand the situation. Think about the implications. Put yourself in the customer's shoes. Analyze the root of the problem. Ask appropriate questions to make sure you have a complete understanding of the situation.

Respond with an effective solution. Develop a solution that will meet your organization's requirements and satisfy the customer's need.

Finding Solutions

Xtra Leasing, a trailer leasing company in St. Louis, had leased hundreds of trailers to a particular customer. Somehow a defect was spotted in some of the new trailers. The lug nuts on the wheels would loosen and fall off, and then the wheels would come off while the truck was in motion, creating a very dangerous situation. After some research, it was determined that the problem was not the fault of the leasing company, but of the manufacturer.

The leasing company went to the manufacturer with the problem. After looking into the situation, the manufacturer admitted the problem, but said only 10 percent of the wheels were bad, and that is all they would take care of. However, the leasing company had a better appreciation of its obligation to the customer. It replaced *all* of the wheels on *all* of the vehicles for this client. The leasing company took more responsibility than the manufacturer would. It went above and beyond the call of duty. Taking responsibility for this problem cost Xtra a lot of money in the short term. In the long term, however, the customer's renewed confidence was overwhelming. It helped to solidify the relationship with the customer. Xtra turned a Moment of Misery into a Moment of Magic.

Another company that solved a huge, potentially catastrophic problem (which was not its fault) was Johnson & Johnson, with the Tylenol scare back in 1983. Someone had broken open Tylenol packages and laced the capsules with cyanide. Johnson & Johnson immediately pulled all Tylenol from store shelves nationwide. In the short run, it cost them dearly. In the long run, it paid big dividends. Trust is essential to anyone in the pharmaceutical business; people are not going to take a medication they can't trust. Johnson & Johnson increased the confidence of the public by acting thoroughly and decisively and in the interest of its customers.

CREATIVE SOLUTIONS

Years ago, I became interested in a four-wheel-drive sport-utility vehicle. I had made several trips to the showroom to admire the vehicle's sturdy, outdoors appeal. The model I wanted carried a hefty price tag, one that put it in the same range as many luxury cars.

When I began serious negotiations with the salesman, we ran into a snag. One thing I really wanted was a free loaner car anytime my vehicle went in for major service. I was aware that a number of other automobile dealerships offered their customers this arrangement. I asked the sport-utility vehicle dealer if he could give me a free loaner while my car was being serviced. He said, "No, we don't do that. It's not our policy." I told him his competition was willing to do this. He asked who I was referring to. I told him about three other automobile dealers' service policies. He said the other cars were more expensive. They could afford to give the loaner. I told him he should check out his competition. Two of the dealers had cars starting at very aggressive prices – prices that had nothing to do with the luxury segment he seemed to think those dealers offered.

A possible solution for this salesperson would have been to raise the price offered on the sport-utility vehicle to cover any rental costs. I would have paid more to have a service I consider important. Because the dealer couldn't be flexible enough to find a creative solution, he lost my business.

These kinds of problems can become Moments of Magic if they are handled properly. Recently my wife and I had our kitchen remodeled. The contractor made two mistakes, both of which were corrected effectively. First, he installed the wrong kind of Formica. We had specified a certain grade of Formica for the countertops, called ColorCore. Standard Formica has a brown edge, covered with a color laminate. ColorCore is the same color all the way through, with no brown edge. The contractor accidentally ordered standard Formica. After realizing his mistake, he offered to sell us the standard Formica for a substantial discount. However, because our countertops were light gray, the brown core detracted from the appearance, and my wife insisted we go with ColorCore. The contractor admitted his mistake, and absorbed the cost of replacing the Formica without hesitation.

Our contractor's second mistake occurred in building a space for our refrigerator. In error, he measured the space to fit a certain high-end type of refrigerator called Sub-Zero. It takes up less space because the condenser is on the top instead of the back. When we tried to move in our standard refrigerator, guess what happened? It didn't fit. We faced a Moment of Misery. He would have to rip apart half of the kitchen to fix this problem. What did he do? He found a creative solution. He sold us a Sub-Zero refrigerator at a substantial discount. He avoided having to redo the kitchen, and we got the high-end refrigerator we had eventually hoped to buy anyway at a very good price. Everyone was happy.

Similarly, employers can find creative solutions to fit the special needs of employees. Consider the case of a single mother with young children. She wants to leave work early to take care of her children after school. Perhaps the employer can allow her to adjust her schedule with flexible hours, making up time on Saturday, or arrangements could be made for her to do some of her work at home after her children have gone to bed. Many companies have now embraced these "Flex Time" arrangements.

RECOGNIZE PROBLEMS

Sometimes your customers don't tell you about a problem. You just have to recognize that there is one. Years ago, a simple concept of prepared meals solved the problem for consumers of a major grocery store chain. The grocery company's executives realized that there were more and more double-income families. The tradition of one "breadwinner" and one "homemaker" was changing. The problem was pretty straightforward: who would make dinner if *no one* stayed home?

Convenience was the solution to the problem. The company hired chefs to work at each store to prepare ready-to-eat meals that were healthy and nutritious, but most of all, tasted good. Their meals ranged from individual portions to large roasted chickens. All that the customers had to do was pick up the meal on the way home from work and reheat it when they were ready to eat.

Someone once said, "Problems create opportunities." Perhaps a better, more positive word for "problem" is "situation." Analyze the "situation" and deal with it. Turn the "situation" around and make it an opportunity to show how good you and your company are.

In most cases, if you do business with a customer long enough, you will eventually face a "situation." It is how you handle these situations that will keep customers coming back. Let them know they can count on you. And when a Moment of Misery happens, they know that you will make it right and turn it into a Moment of Magic.

Magic Hints!

- No matter how knowledgeable and enthusiastic you are, if you do not solve the problem you will not satisfy the customer.
- Listen carefully to what the customer says. Make sure you understand the situation before you take action.
- Respond quickly, decisively and thoroughly, so you can maintain the customer's confidence.
- Use creative problem solving to find "win-win" solutions. Be flexible. Do not be limited by policy or past practice.
- Be willing to bend the rules as long as it does not hurt the business.

The following link will lead you to more magic hints including articles, videos, and tips:

www.MomentsOfMagicBook.com/chapter9

Or Scan:

CHAPTER 10

Be Reliable

"This is the earliest I have ever been late."

—Yogi Berra to Joe Garagiola

Benjamin Franklin said, "In this world nothing can be certain, except death and taxes." Indeed, sometimes it may seem like there are very few people or institutions in life on which we can rely. Sometimes the problem just does not get fixed or it takes repeated phone calls to get an answer.

That is why it is so very important for you to prove to be reliable in how you handle your customers' questions, problems and complaints.

Reliability is the appliance serviceman who was scheduled to come to my house the day a heavy snow was forecast. He called the day before to let us know that he would try to keep his appointment with us in spite of the snow.

Reliability is the hotel where I can stay and always receive a good room and excellent service. If and when problems arise, the team has proven consistently that it will take care of those problems.

Reliability is the fellow employee you can call upon for information or help and can count on to have the material to you within a short time that afternoon, the next day, or whenever promised.

Being reliable starts with your attitude. Reliable people do "whatever it takes" to get the job done. If they must stay 30 minutes late, or work through lunch, they do it. If they have to rearrange priorities, they do it. They make the extra effort. They view their jobs not in the clock-puncher mentality of "I can't wait until the day is over," but instead, "I enjoy what I am doing, and I'm going to have a great day helping people." They do what they do because they want to, not because they have to.

Dennis Waitley attacks those who carry the "Thank God It's Friday" attitude. He suggests we say instead, "Thank God it's Monday" and focus on all the positive things we are going to accomplish with our week.

Zig Ziglar tells a story about a group of men working in a railroad yard. A limousine drove up and a well dressed man got out. He walked over to one of the workers and said, "Hi, Charlie, how are you doin'?" They exchanged pleasantries, and then the man got back in his limousine and drove away. The worker's colleagues asked what that was about. The worker said, "That's my friend Bob. He is president of the railroad. We started here at the same time, 25 years ago."

A co-worker asked, "How come he's president of the railroad, and you're working here in the yard?"

The worker answered, "Twenty-five years ago when we started here together, I went to work for a paycheck. He went to work for the railroad."

That is the attitude of dedication we must take. The worker was reliable in that he showed up for work every day. But the president did much more. He immersed himself in the business.

Reliability can be summed up by asking this question:

How easy and desirable are we to do business with?

If someone is easy and desirable to do business with, you know he or she will always accommodate your needs. They are accessible, flexible and accountable and always follow through. Here are tips on how you can become more reliable:

BE ACCESSIBLE

That is the first requirement for being easy to do business with. If people cannot find you, they cannot bring their demands or needs to you. For a business, this means having hours that suit your customers. It may mean toll-free telephone service, perhaps with operators on duty in the evenings and on weekends. It means having a user-friendly website. It means having enough service people on the floor to handle the volume of customers at peak times. It also could mean having various locations around town, so people do not have to drive far to do business with you. It could mean taking your program or service to the customer's location, such as the way the Red Cross teaches first aid or CPR classes in workplaces.

For employees, accessibility is equally critical. Avoid unnecessary absences from your office, so people can find you if they need you. When you are out of the office or on the phone, have a secretary or voice mail take your messages. Return phone calls, texts and emails as soon as possible. Do not prolong meetings. Consider an "open-door" policy.

If you are on a hot project, give key people your home telephone number. When you travel or leave the office, provide a number where you can be reached.

BE FLEXIBLE

Do what it takes to get the job done. Avoid the attitude of, "We've never done it that way before," or "That's not policy."

If your customer needs something right away that can't be faxed or emailed, courier or ship it. If he or she needs it the next day, send it by overnight express.

Accommodate reasonable requests. If the customer asks you to have a meal ready at noon for pickup, do it. If the request is for a club sandwich without bacon, leave off the bacon.

In the 1970 movie *Five Easy Pieces*, Jack Nicholson walks into a diner and asks for whole wheat toast. The waitress says, "We don't serve whole wheat toast." Nicholson says, "I know you have whole wheat toast, because you serve a chicken sandwich on whole wheat." She continues to refuse, so he asks for a chicken sandwich, but hold the chicken, lettuce and mayonnaise. He pays for the chicken sandwich just so he can get his whole wheat toast.

Several years ago, I was buying a home. Even though I could afford it, I was having great difficulty getting a loan since I was self-employed. Bankers were scrutinizing my business income and my business plan. One day, I read a commentary by Mark Vittert in the *St. Louis Business Journal* about how people don't do business "on a handshake" anymore. The article was about a time when integrity and trust were major parts of doing business and people did not rely just on information on a form. That same day, I ran into a banker named Hord Hardin. I explained my situation, and he listened.

We made an appointment to talk about the loan. I filled out the forms, showed him my tax returns for the last two years, and presented my speaking engagement calendar. The bank gave me the loan on the spot. There was never a late payment, and the loan was paid off early. Hord Hardin was willing to have a little faith in me, and do business "on a handshake."

Follow Through

The late Robert Schuller said, "Those who fail, fail to follow through."

If you say you are going to do something, do it. If you say you will email the information, email it. If you say you will have the project done by Monday, get it done. Or if there is a good reason it is not done, let your customer know what is going on.

Sometimes, salespeople are not good at following through. They are good at building excitement, but not at the nitty gritty work. Following through often is a series of basic tasks. Keeping promises to our customers is essential to building trust.

One person who followed through was the man who sold me a car years ago, a gentleman named Harl White. I'll never forget him. While making the deal, he was always reliable and dependable. Whenever I needed service, he arranged for a loaner. One time, I had my car in for service, and was given a compact car as a loaner. That would have been fine, except that I was picking up three clients at the airport later that morning. I needed something a little bit larger. I presented the problem to Harl, and he loaned me his demonstrator, a brand new top-of-the-line Mercedes! He certainly impressed me...and I certainly impressed my clients!

BE ACCOUNTABLE

If something goes wrong, stand up and face the situation. Take responsibility.

The staff of the Ritz-Carlton hotels provides a wonderful example of accountability. One of the rules of the Ritz-Carlton is that whenever a customer presents a problem ("opportunity" in Ritz-Carlton language) to an employee, it is that employee's responsibility to see that the "opportunity" is resolved.

If a guest wants directions to the banquet room, the employee will walk the person there, rather than just give directions. If a guest goes to a bellman and says a light in the room is broken, it is the bellman's responsibility to get the light fixed. The bellman may need to call maintenance or housekeeping to do the actual work, but the bellman will follow through to see the work is done. The bellman will then contact the customer to make sure the problem has been resolved to his or her satisfaction. In other words, the bellman owns the problem.

Here is another example of how the Ritz-Carlton gives extraordinary service. A guest arrived in town late one night. He did not have a reservation at the Ritz, and the hotel was full. The clerk at the desk checked another hotel two blocks away. It had a room, so the Ritz booked the man there. The bellman then drove the man and his luggage to the second hotel. But that's not the end.

It was midnight, and the man was hungry. The bellman knew this. He also knew that the second hotel's restaurant and room service had closed for the night. So he ordered a meal from the Ritz's room service. The Ritz's room service delivered the meal to him – two blocks away.

Needless to say, he spent the next few nights at the Ritz. The Ritz did not have to take care of this guest, since he had not guaranteed a room for late arrival. But the Ritz staff took control of the situation and turned it into an opportunity to win the customer's confidence. They demonstrated 100 percent accountability.

Neiman Marcus is another company that empowers its employees with a wide range of accountability. Neiman Marcus employees do not just work in one department. They are able to sell in all departments. One of its very best employees works in the St. Louis store. His name is John Bullock. In an earlier chapter, John was noted as an example of someone who knows his business. John also is a good example of someone who is very reliable and accountable. You can depend on him to follow through.

When I got married, I was looking for a gift for the groomsmen. I found a leather address book at the Neiman Marcus store where John was working. The problem was the store only had one book. John said he would make sure I had these gifts and not to worry. He called other stores around the country; he had to go to six stores to get the seven books I needed. Today, when the St. Louis Neiman Marcus store trains new employees, John Bullock is presented in the training session as an example of what a good Neiman Marcus employee does.

Webster's Dictionary defines reliability with words such as "dependable and trustworthy." No matter how good you are, or how good your price is, it may all come down to whether or not your customers can rely on you. A few years ago I heard an advertising salesman of a small public relations firm tell his client that he could have his project finished with excellent quality, great speed and at a low price, but the client could only have two of the three.

Today, that salesman would lose his client. Those options should be standard and probably are the client's expectations. The only variable might be the price.

Be reliable. It can be your competitive edge.

Magic Hints!

- Reliability is proving to your customers that they can count on you.
- Test your reliability by asking these questions: How easy are we to do business with? How desirable are we to do business with?
- Make sure your customers can reach you. When you are not in your office, make arrangements for callers to reach you or leave messages.
- Be flexible to accommodate special or urgent requests.
- Carry out every promise you make.
- Be accountable. Take responsibility.
- Reliability and accountability can be your competitive advantages.

The following link will lead you to more magic hints including articles, videos, and tips:

www.MomentsOfMagicBook.com/chapter10

Or Scan:

CHAPTER 11

Appreciate Your Customer

"Remember that a man's name is, to him, the sweetest
and most important sound in any language."

—Dale Carnegie

Each of the suggestions so far has dealt strictly on a business
level. The final of these five ways to create Moments of
Magic goes beyond "strictly business" and into the realm
of the personal. This is appreciating the customer.

Everyone needs to be told he or she is important. People thrive
on praise. We all like to feel appreciated. You can create Moments
of Magic with your customers when you respond to their basic human needs for recognition.

Take an interest in your customers as people. Use their names
in conversation. Have fun with them. Recognize significant occasions. And most importantly, say thanks.

TAKE AN INTEREST IN YOUR CUSTOMERS AS PEOPLE

Most people have a life away from their work. They have families, friends and hobbies and they enjoy leisure activities.

Get to know your customers. In a 30-second telephone conversation, you may just chat about weather in your part of the country versus theirs. In a long-term client relationship, you may become close friends and socialize with your customer away from work.

Famous businessman and author Harvey Mackay has a form he calls the "Mackay 66." This is a questionnaire that has questions ranging from the customer's business needs to the name of a spouse. Smart business people know that a business relationship also is a personal relationship. The people must get to know each other so they can begin to work well together.

That is why companies hold retreats for their staffs. That is why company social events like picnics and bowling leagues are beneficial. They build working relationships. They help us see each other not just behind the desk, but as people.

Lunch is a great way to get acquainted with your customer in a more relaxed way. Salespeople take clients to lunch. Bosses take employees to lunch.

As you get to know your customers, you will find out what is important to them: their children, a hobby or a cause. You will learn about significant events such as births, marriages and graduations. You can share your congratulations at joyous occasions and your sympathies at negative events.

RECOGNIZE THE CUSTOMER BY NAME

What is the favorite word all of us like to hear? Our own name!

Selective use of the customer's name can add sparkle to your relationship. It reminds the customer you are talking directly to him or her, and not anyone else. On the phone, it can be very helpful to intersperse periodic "Yes, Mr. Jones" statements. At Venture discount department stores, the checkout clerks read the customer's name off of the credit card or check and say, "Thank you, Ms. Smith."

It is a pleasure to visit a fine hotel and be greeted by name every time you pass through the lobby. When my wife and I stayed at the Watergate Hotel in Washington, D.C., the people at the front desk greeted us by saying, "Mr. and Mrs. Hyken, it's so great to have you here. Is this your first time at our hotel? You're going to love it. We have a special room just for the two of you."

Three hours later, we were ready for dinner. As we passed through the lobby, we were greeted again, "Good evening, Mr. and Mrs. Hyken. Have a great night out." This is the difference between a company that teaches people to care and a company that teaches people to simply be clerks.

HAVE FUN WITH YOUR CUSTOMERS

You can build relationships by having fun with your customers.

Salespeople take their customers to professional sports events. At Halloween, retailers allow their employees to work in costume. One grocery store lets customers vote for their favorite checker.

On Southwest Airlines, flight attendants frequently will do fun things during flights. Some have even been known to do magic tricks.

Sharing a good joke or story is a good way to have fun with your customers. Another way is to share pictures or mementos of family events or vacations.

RECOGNIZE SIGNIFICANT OCCASIONS

At the end of the year, businesses typically send holiday cards to their customers. This is a good idea. It keeps the company name in front of the customer and is a great way of saying thanks. Many bosses send individualized cards to employees. This provides an opportunity to thank the employee for the year's efforts.

Why not take this a step further? Why not send a card for the customer's birthday? Or the anniversary of your doing business together? Jim Rhode has designed a marketing program to help dentists build their practices. He calls it event marketing. His clients not only send traditional holiday cards to their customers, they also send birthday cards and Valentine's Day cards.

All of us like recognition on our birthday. No matter how gruff or indifferent an exterior one may project, we all have a soft spot for a birthday celebration that happens to be ours. People may say they are too old and do not want to remember, but that is hogwash! Not only does Jim recognize these types of events, but he also has his dentists send out regular postcards to help educate customers about dental care, and help them overcome fears of going to the dentist. Peanuts characters (Charlie Brown, Snoopy, Lucy, etc.) on the cards help to humanize the cards and add a light touch.

Say "Thanks"

One word you can never say often enough is "thanks."

Thank your customers for doing business with you. Thank them for their ideas and anything they may have shared with you. I always appreciate receiving thank-you cards.

A meeting planner I know, Jim Nagel, has a card with the words "thank you" written repeatedly on the front of it. On the inside it says, "A million thanks." I liked the card enough that I asked him if I could borrow the design and print my own supply. I went through my first thousand in just over a year!

I carry a stack of the cards wherever I go. After I am finished with a speech, I may write several notes on the airplane during the trip home.

A few years ago, one of my clients offered me a full-time job, paying a healthy six-figure salary. I asked why they offered me the job. They said it was because of the thank-you notes I wrote. They said, "You've worked for us six or eight times over the last couple years, and every single time you get together with us, whether it's for a speech or to take you to lunch, you always write these little thank-you notes. They're so nice, it makes us feel like you really care about us and you really care about our business. You do little things above and beyond the call of duty. We had an employee Christmas party, and you came and did a magic show and didn't charge us. If you could teach this attitude to the rest of our employees, you would be a very effective leader."

"Thank-you" can also be said in a large scale way. My financial planner holds an elegant holiday party every year for his clients. Some companies have large employee picnics and special events. Each year, on the last home game of the season, the St. Louis Cardinals baseball team holds "Fan Appreciation Day." Anyone who buys a reserved seat for that last game of the season receives a coupon good for a free ticket to any home game of the next season!

Ringling Brothers said thanks in a big way during the circus's 100th anniversary. Any child born during the anniversary year could receive a free ticket to the circus, good anytime during the child's lifetime.

There are some special ways to say thank you and recognize employees, volunteers and other special groups. Awards and mementos can be given to all who contribute to a special project. Annual luncheons or dinners can provide a group thank-you and recall the accomplishments of the past year. Dressing up for an elegant banquet meal makes people feel special.

Appreciate the customer! My friend Dr. Larry Baker says, "The most abused customer is the sold customer." Don't take your customers for granted. Let them know they are important.

Magic Hints!

- Remember, we all like to be told that we are important.
- Say "thank you." Write thank-you notes and say "thanks" in person.
- Make time to visit informally with your customers and get to know them as people.
- Recognize your customers by name.
- Do fun activities like sponsoring contests, dressing up in costume, or sharing jokes and stories.
- Recognize significant occasions like Christmas, Hanukkah, birthdays, business anniversaries, and others.
- One word you can never say enough is "thanks."

The following link will lead you to more magic hints including articles, videos, and tips:

www.MomentsOfMagicBook.com/chapter11

Or Scan:

"In the long run, no matter how good or successful you are or how clever or crafty, your business and its future are in the hands of the people you hire."

—Akio Morita,
Co-founder, Sony

PART III

Putting Moments of Magic to Work

S tudy and practice the five steps it takes to make magic, along with the five ways to create Moments of Magic.

Once you have mastered these skills, you are ready to face the biggest challenge in customer service: the irate customer. Following are some suggestions for handling complaining customers.

Another step in utilizing the Moments of Magic concepts is getting support throughout the organization. Even the best customer service program will not work unless it is supported by top management and by all employees.

CHAPTER 12

Handling The Complaining Customer

"There is only one boss – the customer. Customers can fire everybody in the company from the chairman on down, simply by spending their money somewhere else."

—Sam Walton

Without a doubt, one of the single most important moments of truth is when the customer complains. More than any other time, that is when we put our reputation on the line.

We can turn complaining customers into our friends, or we can turn them into our enemies. Often, there is not much middle ground. A customer complaint represents a dramatic turning point in the relationship between the customer and a business or organization.

Keep this in mind: we want our customers to complain when they are not happy. We want them to expect good service from us. My buddy Phil Wexler says, "We want our complaining customers to become demanding customers."

Why Handling Complaints Is Important

We have often heard such statements as, "I had to call ABC Company three times before they straightened out my problem," "I sat on hold for 10 minutes before someone answered," or "They kept trying to convince me it was my problem and would not take responsibility for what they screwed up."

If you have been treated that way, you are not going to be happy. And if you are not happy, you are going to tell your friends. The White House Office of Consumer Affairs commissioned the Technical Assistance Research Program to do a study of customer complaints. The study showed that for every complaint, the complainer will tell an average of 10 other people about the situation. A segment of complainers, 13 percent, will tell more than 20 people. If people are upset, they will talk about it. And these days, they will likely talk about it on social media platforms, to a potential audience of millions!

By leaving one person unhappy, you actually are creating negative publicity about your organization for at least 10 people and probably far more. Many recent studies confirm that this is true! Maybe you can afford to lose one customer. But can you afford to lose 10 customers? A hundred? A thousand?

Here is more food for thought: that same study determined that for every customer who complained, 25 more people have complaints but did not come forward. What does this mean? For every one person who complains to you, there are another 25 people complaining to their friends, their parents, their kids, their cousins – everybody. In other words, 96 percent of the people out there who have a complaint are not talking to you.

No matter how loyal your customers are, you eventually will lose them if you do not address their complaints. Charlie Mudd tells a story he calls "The Wile E. Coyote Syndrome" at his company's sales meetings. In the "Road Runner" cartoons, Wile E. Coyote constantly destroys himself with Acme products. Whether it is dynamite, a truck or a ball, the Acme product never works. The dynamite blows up in the coyote's face. The truck crashes into the mountain because of bad brakes, and so on. But he keeps going back to Acme Company for these faulty products. Now one day, he is going to wise up and realize that Acme is not a good deal. He is going to go to another supplier.

The same thing will happen to your customers if you fail to service them. Unhappy customers may continue to do business with you for a while, but they will eventually stop and take their business elsewhere.

The good news is that you can win over your customer with good service. If customers complain, and you jump through hoops to take care of them, they will be your customers for life. And they will tell 10 other people that you took care of them. They will be your best public relations.

Is the Customer Always Right?

Some people believe that the customer is always right. I disagree. Customers are not always right, but they are always the customer.

Sometimes customers can be irate, demanding and unreasonable. Just because we believe in serving the customer does not mean we must give in to every demand. If we have to operate by the rules and policies of our organizations, we may not be able to be as flexible as necessary. However, if the customer is not reasonable, we may not want to be flexible. We need to be helpful and work out a solution.

There are extreme examples of saying the customer is always right. For example, the president of Nordstrom's department store brags about a customer who brought in a set of tires that were worn out and bald. The customer told the clerk the tires didn't perform well, and he demanded a refund (without a receipt, of course). The store gave him his money and took back the tires. There is one wrinkle: this store does not sell tires! It doesn't even have an automotive department!

It's a famous story, and I know the Nordstrom's example shows how far the company will go to make a customer happy. But is it reasonable?

Here is an alternative strategy that might have served the interests of both the store and the customer. First, explain to the customer that the store does not sell tires and never has. Then, help the customer find a store that does sell tires, perhaps the brand that he has the problem with, or maybe even the store where the tires were originally purchased. That would have helped the customer without incurring an unjustified expense for the company, while leading the customer to a place that really could help him. That said, the way Nordstrom's handled this particular customer is why it is a legend in the customer service industry. The publicity received as a result of taking care of this customer, however unreasonable the request might have been, was well worth the price of the four tires. When customers are wrong, and they sometimes are, we should attempt to educate them. Explain the situation without being offensive. Help them understand and come up with a reasonable solution.

THE THREE RESPONSES

There are three ways of responding to customers: defensive, aggressive and helpful. When presented with a complaint, our instinctive response is to defend ourselves. If your spouse asks you why you were late, you may defend why you were late. This defensive response is similar to how some people respond when confronted by a customer. Defensiveness is not the best approach to handling customers, but it is an approach people use over and over.

When people become defensive, they "backpedal" and make excuses. They rationalize their mistakes or other people's mistakes. They do not want their company to look like the bad guy. In essence, they are saying, "We're not wrong. You're wrong."

The defensive posture is rigid. It limits itself to just explaining to the customer why things were done a certain way. "This is our policy. We do not provide delivery outside of a three-mile radius. I am sorry. The salesman told you something we cannot do."

A variation of defensive behavior is aggressiveness. This posture attempts to change the customer's mind. "There is nothing wrong with this car. All of our engines make that clanking noise."

The customer may not always be right, but he or she deserves to be listened to. There is a hotel I regularly use for seminars. My seminar normally starts at 8 a.m. with coffee service beginning at 7:45 a.m. For one particular seminar, we moved back the starting time a half hour to accommodate the hotel's request. The hotel needed the room for an evening function, and it would help them for us to be out at 5 p.m. instead of 5:30 p.m., our usual ending time.

That morning, I arrived at 7 a.m. The contract for the meeting said coffee would be brought out by 7:15 with the seminar to start at 7:30. The time came, and there was no coffee. I found a catering employee and asked where my coffee was. I was told no, this could not be done. The paperwork for catering said 7:45 coffee, 8 a.m. seminar, the usual schedule. Someone at the hotel had not changed the paperwork.

The employee insisted there was nothing he could do. He had to follow what was on his paperwork. We insisted that he follow our contract. When he refused, I said I would get the coffee myself. He said no, and it became a confrontation. That should never have happened. While humans make mistakes and that is understandable, something in writing such as this should easily have been fixed.

AGGRESSIVENESS BECOMES OFFENSIVE

Another Moment of Misery came from a certain restaurant where I had decided to take my mother to lunch. After a short wait, we were seated. A few minutes later, the hostess came over and said, "You can't have this table."

I said, "My mother and I have already sat down. We are here."

She replied, "I didn't realize it, but the owner is here. He made a reservation for this table."

Now, this restaurant did not accept reservations. I asked why the owner couldn't sit at another table. Finally, the owner himself came over and asked us to move. I was infuriated at being treated this way, especially with my mother as my guest. But I did not want to make a scene and embarrass her. So I complied with his request…and silently vowed never to return to that restaurant again.

That vow lasted until a persistent friend talked me into making another visit to that restaurant. Unfortunately, my second visit was worse than the first.

My friend ordered a chicken sandwich. The first half of the sandwich was fine. It had big chunks of chicken, and he was pleased. But as he finished the sandwich, he noticed something in the chicken that did not taste right.

When the waitress asked how the meal was, my friend said it was fine although there was something wrong with a few chunks of chicken in the second half of the sandwich. He said he was just passing this on for information, since he already had finished the meal.

About two minutes later, the same owner who had evicted my mother and me from our table during the earlier visit came to our table. The owner asked what was wrong with the chicken, and my friend explained.

The owner responded, "There's nothing wrong with our chicken. I made that chicken myself." My friend reiterated that something was wrong, although he was not asking for anything since he had finished the meal. However, the owner insisted on turning the exchange into a confrontation.

I left more disgusted than ever with that restaurant. Believe it or not, another friend prevailed on me, and we gave this restaurant one more try. This day, the special was a half club sandwich and soup. I asked the server what was on the sandwich and was told it had bacon, lettuce, tomato, ham, cheese and mayonnaise. I asked if they could hold the mayonnaise. "Well, I don't know," the server said. A few minutes later the owner walked over. You would think he knew me by now! But he didn't.

He said, "I understand we have a problem."

I said, "We do? I didn't think this was a problem."

"I understand you want your sandwich without mayonnaise."

"Yes, that's right. I do not want mayonnaise."

"This sandwich comes with mayonnaise."

"That's no problem. Just tell the chef to leave it off."

"But it's a *half* sandwich."

"So what?" I asked.

He said, "What would we do with the other half of the sandwich?"

This manager was inflexible and offensive. We got up and left. Next time, no matter how persuasive my friends are, I will never, ever go back to that restaurant.

CREATE AN EMPATHETIC MOOD – BE HELPFUL

When customers bring you a problem, you want them to know that you are concerned and want to solve it.

Showing concern starts by listening. Studies have shown that 85 percent of communication is listening. The customer has contacted you because of a problem, a need. He or she wants to present it and get resolution.

Effective listening is work. Jeff Slutsky writes about a technique he calls the "mirror principle." With the mirror principle, you respond with a portion of your customer's comment. Here's how it works. The customer says, "My computer is broken. When I bought it, I was told it would have a one-year warranty on all parts and labor."

You say, "On all parts and labor?"

And the customer says, "Yes, on parts and labor..."

This lets the person know you are tuned into what he or she is saying.

When you use the mirror technique, it often leads the other person into further comments. In this case, the customer may have gone into a more detailed explanation. "When I was looking at these, I asked about warranty. The salesman said it had a full warranty."

Responding by asking questions is another technique that makes customers feel like they are being heard. "You came here because you felt we could help you, right? Did you bring your copy of the maintenance agreement?"

Another effective listening technique is using the word "we." "It sounds like we missed something here. What can we do to take care of this?"

USE THE "THAT'S RIGHT!" PRINCIPLE

Additionally, a great technique for creating a positive atmosphere with your customer is the use of "That's right!" It brings you and the customer together. It places you and the customer on the same side of the issue. It puts you in a position of being helpful instead of defensive.

"That's right!" is taken from a card trick I learned as a child. In this card trick, the magician leads the audience to pick a certain card. In this example, we will attempt to get the person to pick the eight of hearts. Try this trick for yourself. You will need a friend to help you. Here's a sample of how it might go.

Magician: "How many cards are there in a deck of cards?"

Friend: "52."

Magician: "That's right. Now, I'm going to pick a card, and I want you to guess it. I'm going to write it down. First, in the deck there are red cards and black cards. Would you name either reds or blacks?"

· Friend: "Reds."

Magician: "That's right. Of the reds, there are hearts and diamonds. Would you name either hearts or diamonds?"

Friend: "Hearts."

Magician: "That's right. Now of the hearts, you have number cards and you have picture cards. Would you name either numbers or pictures?"

Friend: "Numbers."

Magician: "That's right. Of the numbers, you have odds and evens. Would you name odd or even?"

Friend: "Even."

Magician: "That's right. Now of the even, you have the 2, 4, 6, 8 and 10 of hearts. Would you name three of those cards?"

Friend: "2, 4 and 8."

Magician: "That's right. Of the 2, 4 and 8, would you name two of those cards?"

Friend: "4 and 8."

Magician: "That's right. Of the 4 and 8, would you name one of those cards?"

Friend: "The 4."

Magician: "And that leaves the 8, doesn't it?"

Friend: "Yes."

Magician: "That's right. You just bought yourself the 8 of hearts!"

Look at the "script" carefully. Notice how the friend answered all of the questions correctly, except for the question: "Of the 4 and 8, would you name one of these cards?" It would have been perfect if our friend would have chosen 8, but he did not. He chose 4. At this point we have a choice in how we respond. We can be pushy, defensive or helpful. Helpful means asking the question… "And that leaves the 8, doesn't it?"

Our friend agrees, and he is back on track. What would have happened if in the beginning we asked our friend to name either reds or blacks, and our friend had said blacks? We want them to say reds. What do we do? We would ask the question…

"That leaves reds, doesn't it?"

Our friend agrees, and he is back on track. Try this trick on your friends. It's fun.

I mention all this because "That's right!" is also a very effective technique for disarming a hostile or irate customer. You use questions to ease confrontational situations. When we truly know our business, we should be able to handle any confrontation with a customer, just by asking the right questions. If your business truly believes in delivering service, and the customer comes to you with a confrontation, start by asking this very simple question:

"Isn't the reason you came to us to do business, because you wanted the quality service for which we have a good reputation?"

The customer says, "Yes." You say, "That's right!" It works wonderfully.

"THAT'S RIGHT!" AT WORK

An airline passenger walked up to the gate agent, very upset that his flight to Los Angeles had just been cancelled. The agent asked the passenger if he knew why the flight was cancelled. The passenger said he didn't.

The agent explained that the plane was found to have bad brakes. The agent did not make excuses, but gave an explanation. The agent then asked the passenger, "You don't want to be on that airplane when it lands with bad brakes, do you?"

"No," said the passenger.

"That's right! You do want to get to Los Angeles on time or as close to on time as possible, don't you?"

The passenger said, "Yes."

The agent asked where he wanted to go. The passenger said, "Downtown Los Angeles."

The agent noted that Los Angeles International is just one of four airports serving metropolitan Los Angeles to which the airline flew. He found a flight to Burbank that left 10 minutes sooner.

"By arriving 10 minutes early, you will make up the extra time it takes to get downtown," the agent said.

The customer was very thankful. A Moment of Misery had been turned into a Moment of Magic.

"That's right!" disarms the hostile customer. You don't say to the customer, "You're right, we're a lousy airline."

That's not true. Instead, you educate the customer in a helpful way. Look at what happened again. The airline agent explained that the flight was cancelled because the plane had bad brakes. Then, he asked the question, "Do you want to be on that plane with bad brakes?" The customer said, "No," and now they were thinking on the same wavelength!

The staff at a hotel used "That's right!" with me when my luggage was lost. They said to me, "We are glad you came to our hotel. We know that the reason you came here is because you know about our ability to take care of our customers. Isn't that true?"

I said, "Yes."

They said, "That's right! And we're not going to let you down." Then they analyzed the situation and solved it.

In this example, note how the employee brought up the positive points of the hotel. He reminded me of its reputation as a good hotel and why I wanted to stay there. This leads us to a very important point about customer service:

We are always selling ourselves and our organizations.

Many people are uncomfortable with the idea of selling. But remember that selling yourself does not mean arm-twisting or manipulation. It simply means bringing up your positive points and keeping those in front of the customer. It can reinforce the customer's desire to do business with you and prevent them from jumping to the competition.

"THAT'S RIGHT!" AND AN IRATE CUSTOMER

Here's another example. The customer has just ordered 100,000 brochures from a printing company. The brochures arrived with smudges. A dialogue could go like this:

Customer: "I've just spent $40,000 to have you print my company brochure. We opened the boxes when they arrived and found smudges all over the cover. We checked the proofs carefully all the way through. I don't understand how this happened. We have a mailing going out the 15th, and we can't use these. I am absolutely livid."

Service representative: "You came to us because you thought we were a good printer, didn't you?"

Customer: "Yes."

Service representative: "That's right. And we've disappointed you."

Customer: "Yes."

Service representative: "That's right. And we don't like to have disappointed customers. Now, let me ask you some questions to find out exactly what is going on. Can you show me a sample of one that is smudged?"

Customer: (Shows sample)

Service representative: "How many are like this?"

Customer: "We have checked about a fourth of the cartons; they're like this in about half."

Service representative: "Your mailing is going out the 15th. How many do you need?"

Customer: "Ten thousand."

Service representative: "If you can find enough good brochures to use for the mailing, go ahead and use those. In the meantime, we will reprint the job."

"That's right!" is part of a general way of thinking that allows us to listen to a complaint, rephrase it and let the customer know you hear it. In a sense, it is showing empathy for the customer.

WHAT TO DO IF NOTHING WORKS

Sometimes, you may try "That's right!" and other ways to listen and respond to the customer. You've shown empathy and sympathy. But the customer remains irate.

There is one more technique you can try. Ask the customer, "If you were me and I were you, and I was coming to you with this problem, what would you do? If you were Acme Industries, how would you handle this situation?" In other words, establish a person-to-person connection and ask the customer to help you work out a solution that is fair, reasonable and realistic.

This tactic proves beyond a shadow of a doubt that you are listening. It may just get the customer to recognize that his or her demands are unreasonable and bring the discussion back to reality.

GIVE THEM A REASON TO COME BACK

You have faced the most irate customer. You have listened. You have built understanding with the help of "That's right!" You have come up with a solution. The customer is satisfied. Everyone is happy. Is your job finished? Not quite. There is one more thing you need to do to cement this customer relationship. Give them a reason to come back.

Solving the problem helps. But it does not guarantee that they will continue to do business with you. If you had a bad meal in a restaurant, wouldn't you think twice about going back, even if they replaced your meal or gave you a refund?

I am a regular customer of TGI Friday's, a well-known national restaurant chain. It has consistent quality and service. However, on one occasion I received a bad meal. That gave me a chance to find out how well the restaurants resolve complaints. I told the waitress my problem, and the manager took the meal off my bill. They also offered me my choice of another meal in its place. That is all well and good. But the manager did something else very important. He handed me his business card. On the back he wrote "Free appetizers and dessert for your entire party on your next visit."

Not only did he resolve the problem, but he gave me a reason to eat there again. He believes in TGI Friday's enough that he wants me to come back to prove that they can do things right.

In a restaurant, that is very important. When you receive a bad meal, your confidence in the restaurant is broken. Replacing the meal or removing the charge helps to ease the inconvenience. But it does not rebuild your confidence and trust. That can only come with another successful visit.

Here's another true story about building up the consumer's confidence. Not long ago, I had a minor service issue with my cell phone – nothing major, just something I needed straightened out. While I was on the phone working this out, the rep asked me an unexpected question: Did I realize that I had never once reached my allotted total of monthly minutes?

Actually, no. I hadn't noticed that! After a few minutes more, the rep suggested a new monthly plan that would cost me a lot less and give me exactly the same service. Wow!

A TALE OF TWO HOTELS

I was staying at a well-known hotel in downtown Atlanta. I arrived late at night. The lobby was beautiful, and the people at the front desk were very nice. I thought I was in for a positive experience because I recognize and appreciate good service.

Unfortunately, once I stepped out of the elevator onto my floor, everything began to go wrong. Little things. The rug was worn. The wallpaper was torn. When I went to turn on the lights, the light switch fell out of the wall. I sat in the chair at the desk, and the leg was broken. I almost fell over.

I called the operator to request a wake-up call because the alarm clock did not seem to work. The phone rang and rang for the operator. When someone finally answered, he put me on hold for a few minutes before he took my request. He sounded like he was having a bad day. Now I was, too.

The next day, my office staff had to call to let me know that they had sent an important fax to me via the hotel's front desk. No one from the hotel had brought it to the room or even called me to say that it had arrived. That was the last straw. I asked to have the manager call me. He never called.

At check-out time, I asked to see the manager. I gave him a list of more than 20 problems I had experienced with the hotel's facilities and service. The manager offered to take about half of the (substantial) nightly rate off my room each night. I accepted that offer, but notice that I walked away without any of the problems being solved. Since the manager could not solve the problems after the fact, what was still missing was an incentive for me to return. Giving me a credit was okay, but it was not a complete solution. They haven't redeemed themselves or shown me they can do the job right. The manager did not offer me any reason to come back!

Next, here is one hotel that did redeem itself. My wife and I stayed at the Ambassador East Hotel on a weekend trip to Chicago. Overall, our experience was very positive.

I like to write on the comment cards they leave in the room and rate the service, especially when it is good service. In this case, everything was nearly perfect. There was only one problem I had noticed. The hotel advertised turndown service, where they turn back your bed covers in the evening, freshen up the room, and leave some type of evening refreshment such as mints or cookies. There was even a flyer on the bed advertising this service. But, when we returned to our room for the night, we had not received the advertised turndown service. This happened for two more nights. It was not a problem or an inconvenience, but I did note it on the comment card, just to let them know. I was not complaining.

Several weeks later, I received a letter from the manager of the hotel saying how sorry they were. "A hotel like ours should not forget those things. The next time you are in this area, stay at our hotel. We will give you the first night free. By the way, we also have a new athletic club."

Nice move. The hotel used this as an opportunity to remind me about its amenities and gave me a reason to come back. Since then, I have gone back, and more than a few times.

Magic Hints!

Be sure to share these tips with your colleagues and others you know.

- We want our customers to complain when they are not happy. We want them to be demanding of us.
- When a customer has a complaint, he or she will tell an average of 10 other people.
- For every customer who complains, another 25 have the same problem but do not complain.
- No matter how loyal your customers are, they eventually will take their business elsewhere if you do not address their complaints.
- The customer is not always right, but they are always the customer. When they make unreasonable demands, we should educate them.
- Three ways of responding to the customer are defensive, aggressive and helpful.
- Defensiveness with the customer is limited to explaining what was done and why.
- Aggressiveness attempts to change the customer's mind.
- The helpful response is centered on the customer's needs.
- Use effective listening skills to create an empathetic mood with the customer.
- "That's right!" is a useful technique to neutralize complaining customers.
- We need to use every contact with the customer as an opportunity to sell ourselves and the organizations we serve.
- Give the complaining customer a reason to come back and do business with you again.
- Provide a complaining customer with a free offer or discount for the customer's next visit.

- Solving the problem is just the first step. Now you must show the customer just how good you really are.
- The customer is not always right, but the customer is always the customer. The customer always deserves to be heard.
- We are always selling ourselves and our organizations.

The following link will lead you to more magic hints including articles, videos, and tips:

www.MomentsOfMagicBook.com/chapter12

Or Scan:

CHAPTER 13

Building a Team Spirit of Service

> "Treat the employee the way you want the
> employee to treat the customer."
>
> —Steven R. Covey
> **Author, 7 *Habits of Highly Effective People***

If your company or organization consists of more than just you, then you need to work at building a spirit of teamwork and service. Everyone in the company needs to display a service-minded attitude.

Good service is an attitude that extends throughout a company. It is a friendly, cooperative, get-it-done attitude. You can feel the magic of this spirit sparkle among everyone you see. On the other hand, a bad attitude can permeate a company too. It is like a black cloud. People shuffle around and seem not to care about what they are doing. When a company pushes its people unrealistically, employees tend to have an attitude and short temper with their customers.

Attitude is important in every part of the company, not just the customer service department. The internal customer is the person inside the company whom you serve in your job. It may be a department to which you deliver reports or the next person in the production process. It may be your boss or the employees you supervise. It all comes down to this:

No matter where you work or what you do, you are in customer service.

To illustrate the importance of internal service within a company, consider the case of a procurement department. Other people in the company come to this department to order their supplies. The people in the department move laboriously slow and give you a "whadayawant" attitude. Do you want to go back there for your supplies? Do you think about ordering your supplies outside on your own? Does the way these people represent your company make you feel proud?

Now, consider the effect of a procurement department staffed with people who are pleasant and efficient. How does that make you feel about your company? Are you more inclined to want to give good service also? When people greet you cheerfully and perform responsively, that inspires you to achieve a higher standard. If you work in a company with upbeat people, you will tend to be more upbeat. You will feel more pride in the company.

Much has been said and written about employee motivation. Programs and buzz words have come and gone. For some, employee motivation is nothing more than posters and slogans. Many times, these types of gimmicks are just superficial band-aids. For the person on the assembly line, posters and slogans about quality are meaningless if the plant is still dirty, supervisors treat employees poorly, and the company emphasizes production above quality.

Service and quality are an attitude. They start at the top echelons of the company. They are carried out in everything the company does. Here are four steps your organization can take to build a winning spirit:

- Create an attitude of service.
- Start this attitude at the top and filter it down.
- Understand employees as customers.
- Give praise.

CREATE AN ATTITUDE OF SERVICE

Like any important commitment, becoming a service-minded company starts with a decision. Yes, we are going to make service our first priority.

This dedication to service should be as fundamental as a company's mission statement. Some companies have incorporated service into their statements of corporate philosophy.

Years ago, Johnson & Johnson's credo helped guide its effective handling of the Tylenol crisis, in which a product tampering incident threatened to destroy the company's brand. Today, that credo still serves as the company's "compass point." When you read this credo, you know that if you are Johnson & Johnson, you cannot skimp or take the easy way out when it comes to the customer.

Johnson & Johnson's Credo

We believe our first responsibility is to the doctors, nurses and patients, to mothers and fathers and all others who use our products and services. In meeting their needs everything we do must be of high quality. We must constantly strive to reduce our costs in order to maintain reasonable prices. Customers' orders must be serviced promptly and accurately. Our suppliers and distributors must have an opportunity to make a fair profit.

We are responsible to our employees, the men and women who work with us throughout the

world. Everyone must be considered as an individual. We must respect their dignity and recognize their merit. They must have a sense of security in their jobs. Compensation must be fair and adequate. We must be mindful of ways to help our employees fulfill their family responsibilities. Employees must feel free to make suggestions and complaints. There must be equal opportunity for employment, development, and advancement for those qualified. We must provide competent management, and their actions must be just and ethical. We are responsible to the communities in which we live and work and to the world community as well. We must be good citizens – support good works and charities and bear our fair share of taxes. We must encourage civic improvements and better health and education. We must maintain in good order the property we are privileged to use, protecting the environment and natural resources.

Our final responsibility is to our stockholders. Business must make a sound profit. We must experiment with new ideas. Research must be carried on, innovative programs developed and mistakes paid for. New equipment must be purchased, new facilities provided and new products launched. Reserves must be created to provide for adverse times. When we operate according to these principles, the stockholders should realize a fair return.

Ritz-Carlton's credo exemplifies the hotel's dedication to service. It is simple and direct.

The Ritz-Carlton Credo

The Ritz-Carlton Hotel is a place where the genuine care and comfort of our guests is our highest mission.

We pledge to provide the finest personal service and facilities for our guests who will always enjoy a warm, relaxed, yet refined ambience.

The Ritz-Carlton experience enlivens the senses, instills well-being, and fulfills even the unexpressed wishes and needs of our guests.

At the Four Seasons, the credo is also simple and compelling: "Do unto others as you would have them do unto you" – also known as the Golden Rule. According to Isadore Sharp, founder of the Four Seasons, "Businesses are all relationships, based on common values, values such as staying true to your word. Every religion also enshrines those values, so you can have different religious beliefs, but underlying those beliefs, you've got people who must have similar values and can work together."

A corporate philosophy or credo should be honored and revered. It should be displayed prominently in company offices. It should be printed in the annual report and the profile brochure. It should be part of the company tradition.

Employees should take the credo seriously. They will do so only if the company also takes the credo seriously, by publishing it, displaying it and living by it. Other statements besides corporate credos can be useful to help focus employees on service. The following statements from Lexus are not corporate philosophies or credos, but are good motivators. These messages are printed on business-card-size stock and are laminated. Employees are encouraged to carry these cards.

The Lexus Covenant

Lexus will enter the most competitive, prestigious automobile race in the world. Over 50 years of Toyota automotive experience has culminated in the creation of Lexus cars. They will be the finest cars ever built.

Lexus will win the race because: Lexus will do it right from the start. Lexus will have the finest dealer network in the industry. Lexus will treat each customer as we would a guest in our home.

If you think you can't, you won't…If you think you can, you will! We can, we will.

As a Lexus Representative I:
L–Listen to the concerns of the Customer
E–Empathize with the Customer's feelings
X–Examine options for a solution
U–Understand the Customer's worth to Lexus
S–Sincerely want to help
C–Communicate the best solution
A–Answer the Customer's questions
R–Respond to the Customer's needs
E–Exceed the Customer's needs
S–"Satisfy the Customer"

Start This Attitude at the Top

Top management must set the example for service. If top management does not practice good service, their words and credos lose all credibility. Good service is practiced in two ways:

1. By the way executives treat customers and the model they provide, and

2. By the way executives treat employees, as employees will not treat customers much differently than the way they are treated.

Employees want to feel valued and appreciated for what they do. When they are charged up and their morale is good, they will produce more.

Upper management should think of itself not as the boss, but as a coach or mentor. A definition of leadership is "getting things done through other people." Good executives don't manage, they lead. They empower people to carry out the responsibilities they are capable of.

Tom Peters advocates a concept called MBWA: Management by Walking Around. Executives should get out of the office and onto the floor. They should visit informally with employees on the job. They should create an atmosphere of mutual respect, not of master and slave. Find out what is going on. Do employees seem happy? Are problems being brought up?

MBWA is a great concept because it keeps management visible. If top management visits the plant only when there are problems, then people will be intimidated when management appears. MBWA disarms uncomfortable feelings by breaking down barriers and helping build a team concept. People are no longer afraid when they see the boss because they are used to the boss being around.

There are other ways to bridge the management-employee gap. One company periodically places its executives in entry-level or line jobs in other departments. The executive is to be treated as a beginner in the job.

This approach has important benefits. First, executives develop insight into the needs of other departments. When they make demands of that department, they have a better understanding of how the department performs its work. Second, the administration becomes sensitive toward lower-level employees because barriers of status and rank are broken down. Finally, this technique is a source of new ideas. Frequently, executives came back with new ideas for both their own department and the department they were visiting. By changing their perspective, they received a fresh view of the company. For example, a sales executive could go into production and ask, "Why are we doing things this way?" It stimulates everyone's thinking from top to bottom.

UNDERSTAND EMPLOYEES AS YOUR CUSTOMERS

In a previous chapter we discussed ways to understand your customers. The same techniques apply for employees. Remember this one-line poem:

Think like the buyer, not like the supplier.

MAINTAIN LINES OF COMMUNICATION

Make sure employees can come to you with problems. Make yourself accessible. Have an "open door" policy. Talk informally with employees and supervisors. Conduct your own informal polls to keep the pulse of employee opinion.

Formal surveys are also useful. These should be done professionally and with strict regard for confidentiality. If employees feel their comments can be traced back to them, they may not be honest about problems.

TREAT EMPLOYEES AS INDIVIDUALS

No two people are alike. Each of us has different needs that we seek to fulfill. It is helpful in the workplace to be aware of personality differences. Myers-Briggs is a popular system for personality profiling. It groups people in four areas: introvert vs. extrovert, intuitive vs. sensing, feeling vs. thinking, and perceptive vs. judgmental.

The classic example is that of a wife who says, "My husband doesn't appreciate me; he never says anything nice to me." This is often due to personality differences in feeling versus thinking. The wife is feeling-oriented and needs more compliments such as, "You are a nice person, you are fun to be around, you really look nice." The husband is thinking-oriented and does not have that need to the same degree. He says, "Why does she always want to hear this? Doesn't she know I love her?"

Turning to the other Myers-Briggs types, an introvert (I) has less of a need to be around people than an extrovert (E). You are more likely to find introverts in computer programming and extroverts in sales. Intuitive (N) people are the idea people. They ask, "What if?" Sensing (S) people deal with the facts in front of them. Accountants are more likely to be sensing, while advertising is a good place to look for intuitives. Judgmental (J) people like time structure and closure. If a project needs to be done by Friday, it will be done. Perceptive (P) people prefer to leave things more open-ended. They say, "Let's wait and see." A "J" office will be neat and orderly with a clear desk. A "P" office will often be cluttered with a wide range of projects and papers, all of which have some reason for being there.

It is important to remember that none of these types are right or wrong. Each has its advantages. Perception and intuition help us to be more creative and consider more possibilities. Sensing and judgment help us deal with the facts before us and take specific action. Each of us has all eight characteristics to some degree. It is most healthy for us to develop our capabilities in all eight areas. If we fall extremely to one end in any of the axes, we may need to work to relate to people at the opposite end.

In companies where Myers-Briggs or other personality typing exercises have been conducted, it is an eye-opening experience. People gain new understanding and appreciation of other employees. They learn why Mr. Smith always drives Mrs. Jones crazy. He is a "Perceptive" and she is a "Judgmental." By recognizing these characteristics, we can appreciate our differences and see the value of different approaches.

Understanding personality types works both ways in the employer-employee relationship. If you are giving a presentation to a detail-minded executive, you need to be prepared with facts and examples. Maybe you should give a formal presentation with slides. For another executive, you may operate more informally. You might give a report over a cup of coffee. The executive says, "Just give me the big picture." He relies on others for the details. Again, neither way is right or wrong.

Get Employees Involved

To build team spirit in your organization, you must get people to think beyond their own jobs. They must be aware of the entire organization and its mission. Encourage them to go to work for the company, not just a paycheck. Remember the function of a business? To get and keep customers. Everyone has a stake in that.

A home remodeling company was having problems in its telemarketing department. Employee turnover was high and morale was low. Money was not a problem; they were well paid. Was it burnout?

I asked the company president how he kept his people motivated. He said they have pep talks. I asked if the telemarketers believe in the product they sell. He was not sure. It was obvious he believed in his product, but the important question was, did the telemarketing department believe in it? These types of telemarketers have an inherently unpleasant job. They call people in the middle of dinner (or whenever), interrupt them and ask them if they need siding, windows or a new roof.

Comedian Jerry Seinfeld has a classic routine on telemarketers. When answering a call from a solicitor, he asks for the solicitors' home number so he can call him back later. When the solicitor refuses to give a home number, he says, "What, you don't want to get calls at home? Well, now you know how it feels." He hangs up. We may not like to receive solicitor calls, and for telemarketers, it may not be fun to make the calls, either.

At this particular company, once the telemarketer produces a lead, he or she turns the call over to a sales representative. The telemarketer has no further contact with the customer. I proposed an idea to the company president suggesting that after the sale is completed, the company have its telemarketers call the customers they produced. They would ask the customers if they are satisfied. Previously, the sales representative had made this follow-up call. This way, however, the telemarketer would have a second contact with the customer and could hear firsthand about how good the company's products are.

The idea worked. Turnover among the top telemarketers dropped sharply. The reason it worked was that the telemarketers got to hear firsthand feedback from the customer. The feedback was good, and the telemarketers had a good feeling about what they were doing.

GIVE PRAISE

Surveys show again and again that a paycheck is just one of many reasons that employees work. Self-fulfillment and a sense of self worth are also strong reasons. Some people quit jobs that pay well because they are not personally satisfying. Therefore, it is important for companies to recognize their employees and let them know they are appreciated. Recognition can be done formally or informally.

FORMAL RECOGNITION

Award and incentive programs are ways to provide formal recognition. If you produce beyond a certain level, you receive a bonus or what some companies call a "President's Award."

Large sales organizations typically have strong incentive programs. Top sellers might receive free trips to Hawaii or Jamaica. Coupled with this is peer recognition. The entire sales force knows that Bill, Juanita, Cleavon and Susan won the trip and the award. Sales awards often are given at annual meetings. Promotions and pay raises are another form of recognition. Smart companies have career tracks and find ways to develop good people. Most companies also give awards for longevity of service.

INFORMAL RECOGNITION

Just as important as formal programs are the informal pats on the back. When the company president sees you in the hall and congratulates you on a great job, it makes you feel good. A certain company has an employee appreciation week. It provides free doughnuts for everyone in the office, gives out roses to employees and hosts a luncheon. Holiday parties and other dinners and socials give informal recognition as well. Employees are treated to a nice meal and get a chance to dress up. The president speaks and thanks everyone for their work during the year. Perhaps there is some humor, such as a roast or a skit about the company.

Informal praise can be summed up by this poem by Helen Lowrie Marshall, from "The Gift of Wonder:"

> **I spoke a word of praise today,**
> **One I had no need to say.**
> **I spoke a word of praise to one**
> **Commending some small service done,**
> **And in return, to my surprise,**
> **I reaped rewards of mountain size;**
> **For such a look of pleasure shone**
> **Upon his face – I'll never own**
> **A gift more beautiful to see**
> **Than that swift smile he gave to me.**
> **I spoke one little word of praise**
> **And sunshine fell on both our ways.**

Build teamwork with your employees. Set an example of good service in how you treat the customer and how you treat the employee. Treat the employee the way you would want the employee to treat the customer. Understand the employee's needs, get employees involved, and respect individual differences. Practice "Management by Walking Around" and keep close to the pulse of your organization. Praise work well done and let everyone know they are important. Remember that every employee has customers, no matter what his or her job. It may be one department, the entire company, or it may be the outside customer. When you create Moments of Magic with your internal customers, it will naturally spread to Moments of Magic for the outside customer.

Magic Hints!

Don't forget to share these with the people you work with.

- Good service is an attitude that extends throughout a company.
- Everyone is involved with customer service, even if they are not dealing directly with the outside customer.
- Corporate philosophies and creeds give a written commitment to service to which everyone can refer.
- Top management must set the example for good service.
- Maintain lines of communication with employees.
- Treat employees as individuals.
- Get employees involved in your business by exposing them to other parts of the operation.
- Give praise through formal and informal programs.
- No matter where you work or what you do, you are in customer service.

The following link will lead you to more magic hints including articles, videos, and tips:

www.MomentsOfMagicBook.com/chapter13

Or Scan:

CHAPTER 14

Conclusion

"Service is a position of power, even of love. I can't understand why more intelligent people don't take it as a career. Learn to do it well."

—John Steinbeck

G ood customer service is not an optional "add-on." It is essential to survival. That goes for organizations and for their individual employees.

Businesses face an increasingly sophisticated marketplace. Consumers have more information available to them than ever before. There is a wealth of advice in the media on how to shop for everything from refrigerators to mutual funds to nursing homes. People know what questions to ask and are less likely to buy with little knowledge.

Customers have learned to expect more. The influx of foreign-made goods in the United States has raised consumer expectations of quality. With these higher expectations, consumers are doing more shopping around. Businesses now request annual bids on printing, insurance and other contracts that once went to the same vendors year after year. Loyalty to vendors is not the same as it has been in the past.

What this means for business is you cannot rest on your laurels. You have to go out every day and prove yourself. You have to keep improving to stay ahead of the competition, and a critical ingredient of success is excellent customer service. Within their organizations, individual employees face a similar situation. More is expected of employees today. In recent years, businesses have shrunk employment ranks through downsizing. Each job is examined for its contribution to the organization and the bottom line. Facing a competitive world marketplace, companies are pressured to keep their costs as low as possible. Employers can no longer afford to carry excess positions.

What does this mean for the employee? One must produce or face the possibility of one's job being eliminated. To keep yourself in good standing within your organization you must pay constant attention to serving your internal customers, including other employees, clients and suppliers with whom you work. Internal customers must be served with every bit of the speed, reliability and quality that we would give to the outside customer. So if you want to stay on top, heed these words:

Pay attention to your customers
(internal and external).

CUSTOMER SERVICE – KEY TO SUCCESS

It is now a non-negotiable essential to give good service to both the outside customer and the inside customer. While I like to describe a moment of good service as a Moment of Magic, there is nothing mysterious about how to create magic with your customers. Anyone can become a maker of magic in customer service.

Good service is nothing more than good business practice. Anyone can learn the tools and skills needed to give good service.

To recap, these five steps can turn you into a maker of magic:

- make a good first impression
- know your business
- be informed: know a little about many things
- be enthusiastic
- understand your customer

In addition, there are five ways to create magic:

- provide quality at every turn
- respond quickly
- solve problems
- be reliable
- appreciate the customer

Most importantly, you must commit yourself to raise your level of customer service. Study each of these 10 steps and practice them. Even start implementing one of them and study the additional readings listed in the Bibliography.

Good service starts with an attitude that your customers are important and making it a priority to take care of them. If you care about what you do, it shows. Put yourself in their shoes and think like the buyer, not like the supplier. Remember that every contact with the customer is a moment of truth. You can turn it into a Moment of Magic.

You are always selling yourself and your organization. Be informed. Talk positively. Recognize your organization's as well as your own attributes and highlight them. Let people know what you do well because no one can represent you better than you. At the same time, be empathetic to the customer. Listen to what they say and think about ways their needs can be better served.

The Moments of Magic concepts work in your personal life, too. Treat your spouse, children, family and friends as you would treat a customer. The same elements of good customer service apply to relationships with the other people in our lives. Respond to their needs and requests on a timely basis. Follow through on your promises and be accountable. Appreciate your family and say "thanks." Think about their needs and how they might be met. Read and study on issues of concern to family and friends. All of these elements go to making good personal relationships. Of course, they go to making good business relationships, too.

Monitor Your Progress

Once you have introduced yourself to the concepts of Moments of Magic, it's time to put them to work. You can use the following checklist to review your progress, and see how good of a maker of magic you have become. Review the checklist periodically to make sure you are not slipping into any bad habits.

Moments of Magic Checklist

- How do you answer the telephone? Is your greeting pleasant and inviting to the customer?
- When you meet customers, do you dress appropriately?
- What periodicals, books, etc., do you read about your business?
- When was the last time you attended a seminar? Do you participate in your professional or trade association?
- Can you name and describe the major events and issues occurring in your community, nation and the world today?
- Do you project an enthusiastic attitude? Do you show other people that you care about your work?
- Do you view work situations with a positive, "We will solve this" attitude?
- Do you ask your customers for their opinions?
- Do you think about ways that your customers' needs could be better met?
- Are you doing a thorough job so your work does not have to be redone?

- Is your correspondence clean, and does it meet or exceed current standards?
- Are you up to date in responding to customer requests?
- Do you take action to resolve customer problems that are brought to you?
- When you make a promise, do you follow through?
- How accessible are you to people who wish to reach you in person or by phone?
- Do you say "thank you" to your customers?
- When you handle a customer complaint, do you provide something that gives the customer a reason to want to do business with you again?
- Does your organization communicate an attitude of service?
- Does your top management set the example for good customer service?

Magic Hints!

Remember, all of the Magic Hints throughout the book are great to share through social media.

- Good customer service is not an optional "add-on." It is essential to survival.

The following link will lead you to more magic hints including articles, videos, and tips:

www.MomentsOfMagicBook.com/chapter14

Or Scan:

SERVICE IS EVERYONE'S BUSINESS

No matter who you are or what you do, you have customer relationships. You have people to whom you provide a product or service in your business life as well as your personal life. A secret of successful people is that they give good, timely service. They have built a reputation. With the help of *Moments of Magic*, you, too, can learn how to give good service. By discovering the secrets of good customer service, you can turn ordinary moments of truth into...

Moments of Magic!

Recommended Reading

Albrecht, Karl. *At America's Service*. New York: Grand Central Publishing, 1995.

Alessandra, Tony Ph.D., Phil Wexler, and Rick Barrera. *Non-Manipulative Selling*. New York: Simon and Schuster, 1992.

Blanchard, Kenneth, Ph.D., and Spencer Johnson. *The One Minute Manager*. New York: Berkley Trade, 2003.

Carlzon, Jan. *Moments of Truth*. New York: HarperBusiness, 1989.

Davidow, William H., and Bro Uttal. *Total Customer Service*. New York: Harper & Row, 1989.

DiJulius, John R. III. *What's the Secret?* New Jersey: Wiley, 2008.

Fromm, Bill. *The 10 Commandments of Business and How to Break Them*. New York: Berkley Trade, 1992.

Hyken, Shep. *The Amazement Revolution*. Austin, Texas: Greenleaf Book Group, 2011.

—*The Cult of the Customer*. New York: Wiley, 2009.

Inghilleri, Leonardo, and Micah Solomon. *Exceptional Service Exceptional Profit*. New York: AMACOM, 2010.

Kriegel, Robert J., and Louis Patler. *If it ain't broke…BREAK IT!* New York: Warner Books, 1992.

LeBoeuf, Michael, Ph.D. *How to Win Customers and Keep Them for Life*. New York: Berkley Trade, 2000.

Leger Marketing. *The Disloyal Company*. Montreal: Transcontinental Books, 2009.

Mackay, Harvey. *Swim with the Sharks without Being Eaten Alive.* New York: HarperCollins Publishers, 2005.

Michelli, Joseph A. *The New Gold Standard.* New York: McGraw-Hill, 2008.

—*The Starbucks Experience.* New York: McGraw-Hill, 2007.

Peters, Tom, and Robert Waterman Jr.. *In Search of Excellence.* New York: HarperCollins, 2004.

Pine, Joseph B. II, and James H. Gilmore. *The Experience Economy.* Boston: Harvard Business School Press, 1999.

Reicheld, Fred. *The Ultimate Question: Driving Good Profits and True Growth.* Boston: Harvard Business School Press, 2006.

Reilly, Tom. *Value Added Selling Techniques.* New York: Congdon & Weed, 1989.

Sanborn, Mark. *The Fred Factor.* New York: Currency Doubleday, 2004.

Sewell, Carl, and Paul Brown. Customers for Life. New York: Crown Business, 2002.

Walther, George R. *Power Talking.* New York: Putnam Publishing, 1991.

Winninger, Tom. *Price Wars: How To Win The Battle For Your Customer.* Minneapolis: St. Thomas Press, 1994.

Order at
www.Hyken.com

The Loyal Customer:
A Lesson From a Cab Driver

This may look like a book, feel like a book and even cost like a book. But, it is not a book. It's a lesson!

This lesson is simple and direct. There aren't lots of chapters with many ideas. Just one very important idea – to create a loyal customer. Through this very entertaining st-ory of a very successful cab driver, you will learn the difference between a satisfied customer and a loyal customer. (The basic story of Frank the Cab driver can be found in chapter one of this book.) Following the lesson there are seven study questions that will take you and your business to a higher level.

64 page paperback book

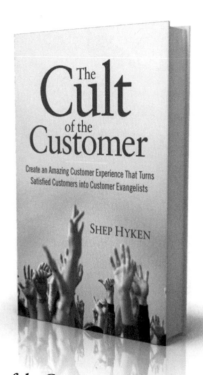

Order at
www.Hyken.com

The Cult of the Customer
Create an Amazing Customer Experience That Turns Satisfied Customers into Customer Evangelists

A *Wall Street Journal* Bestseller!

What is The Cult of the Customer? If you're in business, it's the cult you want to belong to!

The world cult comes from the Latin word cultus, which originally meant "care or tending." This book is about creating a corporate culture that is so focused on taking care of and tending to employees and customers that the culture itself creates *evangelists*. Evangelists are special people who go out of their way to tell the world just how great you and your company are. They are exactly the kind of advocates that you want your organization's culture to create. That's the end result of *The Cult of the Customer*.

There are many companies who have managed to build a culture that reaches this level; a culture rooted in a concept called Amazement. In this book, you'll read their stories, discover exactly how they made *The Cult of the Customer* happen, and learn how you can make it happen, too.

256 page hardback book

Order at
www.Hyken.com

The Amazement Revolution
Seven Customer Service Strategies to Create an Amazing Customer (and Employee) Experience

A *New York Times* and *Wall Street Journal* Bestseller!

What is the Amazement Revolution? It is the culture that can drive any organization—from one employee to tens of thousands—to focus completely on delivering an amazing customer service experience.

Customer service isn't a department—it's a philosophy that includes every person and aspect of the best and brightest companies. In a tough, competitive, and price-sensitive economy, customer service is one of the most essential tools to separate your business from the competition. In this exceptional guide to the principle of amazement, you will read more than one hundred insightful examples from fifty role model companies that teach seven powerful strategies that any organization can implement to create greater customer and employee loyalty. Start your own Amazement Revolution today!

224 page hardback book

About the Author

SHEP HYKEN, is a customer experience expert and the Chief Amazement Officer of Shepard Presentations. He is a *New York Times* and *Wall Street Journal* bestselling author and has been inducted into the National Speakers Association Hall of Fame for lifetime achievement in the speaking profession. Shep works with companies and organizations that want to build loyal relationships with their customers and employees. His articles have been read in hundreds of publications, and he is the author of *Moments of Magic®*, *The Loyal Customer*, *The Cult of the Customer* and *The Amazement Revolution*. He is also the creator of *The Customer Focus™* program, which helps clients develop a customer service culture and loyalty mindset.

In 1983 Shep founded Shepard Presentations and since then has worked with hundreds of clients ranging from Fortune 100 size organizations to companies with fewer than 50 employees. Some of his clients include American Airlines, AAA, Anheuser-Busch, AT&T, AETNA, Abbott Laboratories, American Express - and that's just a few of the A's!

Shep Hyken's most requested programs focus on customer service, customer loyalty, internal service, customer relations and the customer experience. He is known for his high-energy presentations, which combine important information with entertainment (humor and magic) to create exciting programs for his audiences.

Shep Hyken | Shepard Presentations
(314) 692-2200 | Email: info@hyken.com
www.hyken.com